An Eye for **CRICKET**

PATRICK EAGAR
and JOHN ARLOTT
An Eye for CRICKET

HODDER AND STOUGHTON
LONDON SYDNEY AUCKLAND TORONTO

For E.D.R.E.

OPENING PAGE: Prudential Trophy, England v. Australia, The Oval, 1977.

OVERLEAF: Greig, c. Marsh b. Walker, England v. Australia, Edgbaston, 1975.

Designed by Margaret Fraser

British Library Cataloguing in Publication Data

Eagar, Patrick
  An eye for cricket.
  I. Cricket
  I. Title
  II. Arlott, John
  796.358   GV917

ISBN 0 340 24392 9

Contents

Acknowledgments

I would like to thank so many friends all over the world who have helped both directly and indirectly in the production of this book. In particular I would like to thank Simon Guttmann, who showed me what could be done with photography and who will be surprised to see what became of his education; Jim Swanton, whose help and kindness in the early stages were of vital importance; Peter and Ann Short who helped at the right time and almost by accident precipitated a number of visits to Test matches the world over; Peter MacKinnon, custodian of my Australian tripod and chauffeur between Melbourne and Sydney via Wee Jasper; Jan Traylen, who made the original black and white prints for the book; and finally Annabel, whose understanding and patience have made it all possible.

The authors and publisher would like to thank the following for the use of their photographs:

The MCC for their kind permission to reproduce the photograph taken in the Long Room at Lord's.

The Royal Photographic Society, p 8
The Beldam Collection, p 9
The Age, Melbourne, p 10
Fox Photos, p 11
Central Press Photos Ltd, p 12

P.E.

Introduction

In 1963 I bought my first telephoto lens. I remember it well, as it was also the day on which Colin Cowdrey had his arm broken by Wes Hall. I bought it on a visit to London in the morning and then went down to Lord's as a spectator, noticing numerous NO CAMERAS ALLOWED notices around the ground. My new lens was still wrapped up in its box, and the camera to go with it was in my pocket. I had noticed a couple of spectators taking the odd photograph, no doubt as a personal record of a rare visit to the headquarters of cricket. As they had carried out this potentially dangerous manoeuvre undetected, I too succumbed to temptation. One of the first Test match photographs I took was of the moment Cowdrey's arm snapped with a report that sounded like that of a gun.

My first cricket photograph as a professional was taken in 1965, but I had to wait seven years before I could return to Lord's and photograph with official blessing. The agency monopoly was broken for the Ashes series in 1972 – before that, for 40 years or so, all Test matches in England were photographed exclusively by one of two agencies who shared the matches between them. No other photographers were allowed in the grounds. Even in 1972, when perhaps some of the preparations were over-hasty, one of the grounds issued passes to photographers with the words 'Photography strictly forbidden' marked clearly across the bottom.

It was not long after the discovery of photography itself that cricket came to be recorded by the lens. The earliest action cricket photograph is probably that taken by Roger Fenton in 1857 (I include it here with other photographs I admire very much). Fenton is remembered primarily for his graphic coverage of the Crimean War but, for some reason, he was moved to take this photograph of a match between the Royal Artillery and Hunsdonbury. While Fenton was probably more interested in the overall scene, his photograph does illustrate one of the problems that has to be faced by all cricket photographers. The action takes place a long way from the camera, not less than 75 yards and frequently a good deal further. Today we take the telephoto lens for granted but, until the end of the First World War, cameras could not reach out and isolate small groups of players or take close-ups of individuals.

The most famous of the early cricket photographers was George Beldam, Sussex county cricketer, Corinthian footballer and all-round sportsman, who published books of cricket, golf and tennis action photographs between the years 1902 and 1908. He took literally thousands of photographs, posed in the sense that he asked the players to bat or bowl specially for the camera; but, unlike those of his contemporaries, they were genuine action photographs – the ball really was moving. He was able to stop the action by using high shutter speeds and the comparatively fast plates then available to him.

He writes, in *Great Batsmen*, of how he sometimes bowled to his subjects himself, the ball in his right hand and a long electric cord which released the camera shutter in his left. His photographs of Grace, Ranjitsinhji, Fry and

Trumper can still be seen on many pavilion walls and in countless books. The photograph of Victor Trumper (right), possibly his most famous. Original prints made at the time are still in perfect condition and are frequently sharper and clearer than those of today. His attempts at action photographs during matches were not a great success, and one can imagine his frustration at the technical limitations of his equipment.

After the First World War a number of aerial reconnaissance lenses were adapted for use in photographing cricket. The best were the German ones salvaged from zeppelins shot down over England. Two, at least, are still in use today. These long lenses meant that, at last, the cricket photographer could take the previously elusive close-ups from the boundary. The long lenses raised their own problems; accuracy in focusing is critical and they must be mounted very steadily as the slightest vibration at the moment of exposure will ruin a good photograph. Then as now a really good incident that will make a memorable picture may last for only a fraction of a second and may be the only incident worth capturing in the whole of a five-day Test. The photographer must be ready and everything must be precisely right, as there is seldom a second chance. That is no small feat in view of the size and awkwardness of the early telephoto plate camera. Today it is easy to overlook the main limitation. Plates were bulky, heavy and comparatively costly. A photographer would be sent out for the day with a ration of perhaps fifty, the equivalent in weight to a few thousand photographs on today's films.

George Beldam,
c 1902.

Ron Lovitt, 1960.

The old type of camera was still in use in 1960-1 when Australia played West Indies at Brisbane. The excitement of the closing overs meant that those photographers who were still on the ground had used up nearly all their allocation. As the match drew to a climax, shortage of plates became a major problem. It appears that in the final over, when all four results were still possible, only Ron Lovitt of the *Age* and Harry Martin of the *Sydney Morning Herald* were still photographing. They realised that any action would happen very quickly, probably more quickly than they could change over plates (modern motor-driven cameras do not suffer from such disadvantages; several photographs a second are possible). They came to an agreement: Martin would photograph the stroke no matter what happened. He would therefore be looking for the winning run, or would photograph Kline, the last batsman, being clean bowled or LBW. Lovitt, positioned alongside, and to Martin's right, would take the action following the stroke – a catch, a run out or a victory salute.

Hall bowled to Kline, who pushed the ball away on the leg side – Martin took his photograph as planned. Solomon swooped in and threw the wicket down. Lovitt waited that fraction of a second, the mark of a good photographer. The action developed, as Kanhai leapt in the air. That was the moment. A remarkably restrained Lovitt took one of the most famous cricket photographs of all time. Martin, meanwhile, had reloaded his camera and, as some consolation prize, took the players leaving the field.

Willie Vanderson of Fox Photos took an excellent sequence of Frank Tyson bowling at his peak in 1954. All the photographs are very good, but the best is the amazing shot of the follow-through shown here. They were all taken on the same type of camera that Lovitt was to use for the tied Test photograph at Brisbane. The negatives were a vast half-plate. A photographer must observe and analyse a bowler's action. Certain movements are typical of the bowler; some flatter the action; some look ugly and serve little useful purpose. Some bowlers always look good – both Lillee and McKenzie stand out in my memory as being almost impossible to photograph badly. Others need very careful timing indeed.

Dennis Oulds is the doyen of English cricket photographers. His first Test match was in the 1930s and he still works for Central Press on one of the two surviving and currently in use 'long tom' cameras. In all his years photographing cricket he cannot ever remember all eleven members of a fielding side crowding so tightly round the bat as in the final stages of the fifth Test at The Oval in 1968. He took a number of excellent photographs as England sought to beat Australia on a wet Underwood-type wicket, but this one has everything – the dramatically tight field, and the decisive catch as David Brown appears to pick the ball off the bottom of McKenzie's bat.

Cricket photography is a constant juggling act. On the one hand, the photographer should be ready to picture each wicket as it falls – which might be a catch as wide as third slip or gully. On the other hand, he might want close-ups of batsman or bowler, so tight that you can see every stitch in their sweaters. Life being what it is, one has only to decide to concentrate on the bowler to the exclusion of all else, to induce a blood-curdling 'howzat!' from the other end and find that the most dramatic wicket of the day has passed unphotographed. A solution is to use two cameras, one as a permanent long stop, just in case.

A cricket photographer dare not miss even one ball. If he does it will inevitably

Willie Vanderson, 1954.

Dennis Oulds,
1968.

be the one that produces the vital wicket or the most spectacular stroke of the day, a point sometimes lost on one's more sociable friends. I have perplexed many by leaving an excellent lunch long before the end, just because it is five past two. Frequently I have cast a wistful eye at the pavilion or the press box, or what the Australians call 'the outer', to see those who can queue at leisure for something as simple as a cold drink on a hot day, or (more often in England) a hot drink on a cold day.

Many of the best cricket photographs are taken at ground level. This can be a risk as players can get in the way. Even at times we inadvertently encourage it. I have heard captains strategically placing their fields say, 'Back a bit and finer – just over there, by the cameras.' The result is that for the rest of that bowler's spell you will be peering through or around a fielder. Moving cameras and tripods is not always possible on a crowded ground, and it is seldom convenient.

There are times, no matter how hard a photographer tries to concentrate, when things go wrong. In Madras in 1977, John Lever was involved in an unfortunate controversy which became known as the 'Vaseline Affair'. I remember the day well as one of the more tedious days' Test cricket I have photographed. It was very hot, and the interruptions to play seemed endless. The ball went out of shape more often than usual, the players had breaks for drinks and India were struggling

desperately to save the match. So when after lunch yet another interruption to play occurred I, along with the other photographers around the boundary, took this as an opportunity to take a rest. One of us went to find some cold drinks, I took some mischievous photographs of an Indian colleague taking a quick nap, and we all made the most of what appeared to be a welcome break in the intense concentration required to photograph a five-day Test match. It was only later that we discovered to our horror that not one of us had taken a single photograph of the story of the day.

I find there is a strange ignorance among the general public and others, who should know better, about the work of a cricket photographer. Whether out of politeness or mere curiosity I am often asked if I photograph every ball. A moment's thought would show that in a typical Test match the total would exceed 2000 photographs, most of which would be worthless. How then does one know when to take a photograph?

The photographer should follow the match with the same degree of concentration as, say, first slip. The demands on the spectator enjoying a day off from work are considerably less. However, I find that the developing action often gives itself away. Although a piece of action may appear to happen in a moment, intense concentration appears to slow it up. I have been surprised many times while watching the day's highlights in the evening on television – here in the role of spectator – just how quickly some dismissal has happened. In my memory I felt that it had occurred at a much slower pace.

As the bowler delivers the ball, the photographer's eye is on the batsman, usually his face, as a sudden change in his expression can indicate much of what is to follow. A mental note is made of the length and direction of the ball – as long as one is in a position to judge this. A bouncer would immediately indicate a hook, or some evasive action on the part of the batsman; a ball of full length, the drive. If a batsman plays at the ball and misses, there is instant alert – rather like the first pressure on a rifle. After this alert, all attention is on the stumps. If the sun is shining the first clue is often a glint from flying bails – the shutter is released almost without conscious thought.

For a catch behind the wicket or in the slips, there is often a tendency to take the photograph too soon – rather in the way an inexperienced fielder may snatch at a catch. I remember many coaches saying, 'Let the ball come to you.' It is the same for the photographer – let the action happen.

Unfortunately I was never much good at playing cricket myself, and the coaches' advice went largely unheeded. This was probably a disappointment to my father, but he never showed it. I was brought up in a cricket household and could not help developing an affection for the game. So it was natural that my early experiments in photography should include trying my hand at cricket. The immediate problem of access to a long lens on a schoolboy's budget was solved by borrowing my father's binoculars. My first published photograph, paternally accepted by the editor of the *Hampshire Handbook*, was taken by jamming my camera against one half of his precious binoculars.

I am sometimes asked if I get bored with cricket. The problems and the challenges are there every match, and there is always the hope of taking an even better photograph than the one of the day before. Besides, there seems no better way of spending a pleasant summer's day than out on some sunny boundary.

PATRICK EAGAR

The Play

The camera does many things. It can interpret, capture, record; skim a surface or probe a subject; observe, contemplate, analyse, joke, distort, identify, but, above all, it gives evidence: it is the honest witness. There have been many attempts to dispute the adage that 'the camera cannot lie'; but, in fact, it is true; the evidence of the camera is accurate; only, sometimes, the limits of its field of knowledge must be indicated by an interpreter.

In the course of this section, it captures and freezes cricket events often too fast for the eye to follow in definitive detail. If the lens can expose human fallibility, it often illuminates athletic achievement beyond the appreciation of ordinary observation. Sometimes it provides minor evidence on a theme the photographer of the moment did not consider. There is, for instance, a *carte-de-visite* of W. G. Grace in which the eye is instantly caught by his grubby and crumpled shirt; similarly, here, on a level below – or more illuminating than – that of historic event, one might notice Marsh's dirty boots, Boycott's immaculate turn-out.

Memory recalls what the observer's mind conceives to be essentials – which time sometimes magnifies or distorts. The camera, though, records all; and it infallibly dates Patrick Eagar's photographs of the cricketing scene, less in the identities of the players or their clothing – different in every period – than in the social, behavioural and human pattern of their play: these are unmistakably pictures of the nineteen-sixties and -seventies.

By comparison with earlier times – even within the post-war period – they are unique in terms of the uninhibited behaviour, actions, and reactions of the players and spectators. It might be a different game, another world altogether from that of cricket players on the same grounds twenty years ago. Character, approach, bearing are all so altered that, in a catch-phrase, 'Sir Pelham would not recognize it.' Sir Pelham Warner, who saw more cricket than anyone else before or since, and was the personification of Lord's – Establishment – cricket, died in 1963, five months before the first one-day county competition began. As usual, the change at first was so slow as to pass almost unnoticed; it accelerated during the later nineteen-sixties to a degree which would, indeed, have horrified Sir Pelham.

The fundamental cause of the change was honest – even historically inevitable. Simply enough, it was the switch in attitude from the 'the game's the thing', of nineteenth-century public school morality, to a belief that winning was important – even all-important; and a recognition that, if the British cricketers did not recognise the fact, they could expect to spend the rest of their days losing, because other people had certainly become aware of it. Of course the process was gradual; there were some fairly hard competitors in 'the Golden Age'.

The demarcation line in English cricket can probably be drawn in the latter half of the nineteen-thirties. Yorkshire cricketers had always protested that they did not play for fun; and they had already recorded many successes in the County Championship through their strategy and efficiency. In 1933 they acquired a new captain in Brian Sellers; not a great player, though a determined batsman and fearless close fieldsman. At times almost a caricature of the Yorkshireman he wanted to be, once he had found his feet he drove his side hostilely; over-aweing, and all but demolishing, many of their opponents. After the Second World War Wilfred Wooller of Glamorgan and Desmond Eagar of Hampshire reasoned that the strength of their comparatively weak sides could be increased by a high standard of fielding and, especially, of close catching. Their players, keen to improve their performances, accepted the strict disciplines of near-perfect out-

PREVIOUS PAGE:
Greig is dismissed, England v. West Indies, The Oval, 1976.

cricket; slips keeping the backs of their hands on the ground until they moved for a catch, or the ball had gone elsewhere; short leg keeping his eye on the batsman until the last possible moment before he ducked to avoid a hook; outfieldsmen adjusting their position, angle, depth and walk-in rate to each different batsman; mid-off or mid-on receiving returns to the bowler's end.

Wilfred Wooller took Glamorgan to the Championship of 1948 ahead of several otherwise appreciably stronger counties by outstanding close catching. Hampshire won the title in 1961 under Colin Ingleby Mackenzie, but on the basis of Desmond Eagar's training and discipline in the field. Stuart Surridge, in Surrey's historic run, and Jack Bond, captaining Lancashire to their pre-eminence in the one-day game, pursued essentially the same method. Fielding standards rose. Even as late as the nineteen-thirties, Ellis Robinson, standing next to that archetypal Yorkshireman, 'Ticker' Mitchell, in the leg trap, dived a long way to make a catch sprawling on the ground; and, as he stood up and was brushing the dust from his flannels, Mitchell turned to him acidly with, 'Stop mekkin an exhibition o' thysen.' It was unusual then to see mud or grass stains on a cricketer's clothing.

A decade later, Keith Miller at slip, Allan Watkins and Tony Lock at short leg, were throwing themselves hitherto unheard-of distances to make catches. So, too, was the wicketkeeper, Godfrey Evans; but he had, to an extent, been anticipated by George Duckworth keeping to Ted McDonald. Soon virtually anything within diving distance was reckoned a chance.

Keith Carmody, captain of the Australian Services side that toured England during 1945, gave his opening bowlers nine close catchers in the 'umbrella' or 'Carmody' field. His theory was that two or three quick wickets were worth a few fours through the gaps. When county cricket recommenced after the Second World War many counties used extremely hostile fields for the new ball or on difficult pitches. As Brian Sellers had discovered earlier, it was possible to apply psychological pressure by a menacing close field and a generally hostile bearing, so that the batsman felt as though the fieldsmen were breathing down his neck. Up to the inter-war period, the great cricketers could – and did – go on playing into their fifties. Some sides carried as many as two, even three, non-runners, non-benders or non-catchers. Soon, though, it became impossible – especially after the introduction of over-limit play – to 'hide' a man in the field. Now a cricketer is as old as his running. The present generation of players are trained to a degree of physical fitness their predecessors never knew.

At the same time, Sir Alf Ramsey was instilling his lesson of work-rate into footballers. Effect counted, and much of effect stemmed from effort. Belatedly, too, the rewards of the game became more nearly commensurate with the skill and application of the players. The by-products of this creditable improvement, however, have given cause for disquiet.

The first, and most alarming, is the admitted employment of a degree of violence which could easily prove fatal. In January 1975 Peter Lever, whose pace was well short of that of half a dozen subsequent fast bowlers – especially from Australia and West Indies – struck the New Zealander Ewen Chatfield in the head so nearly fatally that, in fact, his breathing ceased and he was only revived by mouth-to-mouth resuscitation. Some years before, Charlie Griffith had hit the Indian batsman, Nari Contractor, in the head only an inch or two from a fatal spot. The warnings have been posted.

No one will deny that, in the past, fast bowlers regarded the short pitched ball as a legitimate threat – even a test of a batsman's nerve. It is true, too, that Larwood and Voce, against Australia in 1932-3, bowled in an intimidatory fashion – called Bodyline – aimed at the batmen's ribs with a close set legside field. No denials, from any quarter at all, can cast doubt on that fact. Now, though, the line of attack has moved, so that while Greig in a recent book described one bowler as aiming accurately 'along the heart line' he dubbed another a 'head hunter'. Dennis Lillee in *The Art of Fast Bowling* says: 'I try to build up a sort of hate feeling against the batsman . . . at the other end of the wicket. It is just a matter of whether you are prepared to be honest about it. The bouncer, or bumper as some call it, is a legitimate delivery sent down short of a length to the batsman with the aim of going through somewhere between the chest and just above the head. The idea is to intimidate the batsman through a fear of being struck by a similar delivery in future, to claim his wicket as he fends the ball off his body with his bat or gloves or, in the case of the compulsive player of the hook stroke, to encourage a catch through a mistimed stroke.'

That, from one of its most brilliant practitioners, is the acceptance of the bouncer as a legitimate item of fast bowling technique. It has led to much bitterness; but it has also proved effective at the highest level. Most countries have employed it, and it has won Test series. Remarkably enough Tyson and Statham did not use it in their successful Australian tour of 1954-5. On the evidence, they did not need it. Now it is an accepted facet of the game; frowned on officially, it seems, rather as a potential defensive tactic in over-limit matches than as a menacing weapon likely eventually to have frightful consequences. The fact remains that it is so generally accepted that a number of batsmen wear helmets as protection against it. That has been condemned by some who are not called upon to face the bouncer delivered by a high speed bowler. Batsmen, though, are permitted leg guards, thigh pads, adbomen protectors – defending parts of the anatomy the bowler rarely seeks to hit – as well as rib padding; why should they be denied the form of protection most likely to save their lives? Similarly dangerous, though not violently intended, is fielding in close-to-the-bat positions. Roger Davis of Glamorgan was all but killed when he was struck by a forcing stroke when standing at short leg. So the crash helmet adds another and, so far, the newest item to the cricket scene.

It is obvious that such unwinking concentration and high-speed reactions as characterise the great fielding sides – each man 'living' with the ball until it reaches its destination – also produce extreme tension. There is, too, little doubt that an appeal – especially the mass appeal – releases tension. Whether it is a spontaneous outburst of pent-up nervous energy or a tactical weapon, the mass team appeal is nevertheless a completely new phenomenon in the first-class game. Photographs taken as recently as the nineteen-fifties show the appeal as a somewhat conversational matter. There have, of course, always been some bowlers – like George Macaulay and 'Tiger' Bill O'Reilly – who shouted their appeals. Most 'asked' quietly; the wicketkeeper might add his voice in the case of a catch at the wicket. There was no suggestion of the nowadays common histrionic mass appeal which has certainly been used by some teams – with one player giving the cue to 'go up' – as a deliberate ploy to unsettle or confuse a nervous umpire. The man who appealed for LBW from square leg or for a legside catch from cover point used to be regarded with half humorous disapproval. Now it is thought in some places that unless the whole side 'goes up', they do not believe the batsman is out. Certainly in recent Test series far more appeals have been made than were justifiable. The extent of the strain can be measured by the retirement of some of the best Australian and West Indian umpires.

The extravagance of present day reactions is magnified by television. Indeed, the media, in general, behave more challengingly than formerly. It is possible, too, that nervous tension is reflected and heightened by a combative hostility. On the other hand, the Australians in recent years certainly gave offence by aggressive attitudes – which showed up badly on television – and swearing. There have always been some cricketers who allowed a dislike of opponents – whether genuine or simulated – to become apparent. Only lately, though, has the majority of a team acted offensively in concert.

The third new manifestation is the emotional response to the fall of a wicket, when half a team will fall upon a successful fieldsman or bowler and embrace him – in sharp contrast to the polite hand-clap of a few years ago. This is unnecessarily embarrassing. As one otherwise hardened player put it, 'I try never to make a catch off x before lunch, I can't bear his morning breath.' The Corinthian footballers gave no more than a nod – at the most a slight handshake – in congratulation for the most important of goals; rugby players, too, maintain an unemotional attitude towards their fellow performers in public.

The effect of the current large rewards for success must not be forgotten. At first-class level the casual – art for art's sake – cricketer is playing fast and loose with his colleagues' living. The man who makes a catch or takes a wicket is contributing to the profit of all; there is gratitude as well as release in the explosion of embraces.

It sometimes seems that the mere presence of the television cameras is a provocation to extravagance in an uninhibited generation. Certainly that is true of spectators, among whom many juniors – but also some adults – seem to find their main pleasure in getting into the picture. Until a few years ago no spectators would have thought of running on to a football or cricket field; indeed, anyone who did so could expect a strong rebuke from the rest of the crowd for interrupting the action.

Now, however, it would seem strange if every development of any importance were not marked by some exhibitionist interrupting play and molesting players. Eventually, there will be some unsavoury incident (the Australian batsmen were jostled by spectators running on to the field when they thought, mistakenly, that Thomson was out towards the end of the Prudential World Cup Final of 1975). The streaker at Lord's, unthinkable a few years earlier, is, unfortunately, not likely to prove the ultimate in crowd interference.

All these electric responses by the players, and the exuberant crowd reactions, of course, make for more dramatic photographs. In the same way, the raised standard of fielding and the extreme tensions and precarious risks of the over-limit game make play the more spectacular. If only for these reasons, these photographs are so vivid as to make much earlier work in the same field seem almost static by comparison.

All in all, in these pictures, the camera is a witness to considerable social, economic and technical changes in a game which has always truly reflected its setting.

On Being Out

The fall of a batsman's wicket is consistently the most dramatic event in cricket. With all its analogies of finality and surprise, it has always seized the imagination of players and spectators; and, therefore, of editors. Thus for years photographers were sent to matches to capture the dismissal of batsmen. Neither is that demand confined solely to the press. Anyone watching the 'highlights' of cricket matches on television could be forgiven for believing that the game consists almost entirely of falling wickets and departing batsmen.

In most of the first-class game, and certainly in Test cricket, the whole atmosphere associated with the fall of a wicket has changed vastly since the late nineteen-fifties. There exists a photograph of Jack Hobbs – bowled out for 80 in a Test Trial – turning away from the wicket, a broad smile on his face and his bat raised in salute to the bowler. Hobbs scored more runs and more centuries than anyone else in the history of the first class game, so he, presumably, could afford to give up his wicket and the chance of yet another century. His scoring achievements, however, suggest that he did not lightly surrender his innings. The impressive quality of the picture is the quietly relaxed air of both batsman and wicketkeeper (no one else is shown) – in striking contrast to the histrionics of some – especially the fieldsmen – of a later generation, in the photographs that follow. Out there at the time, someone no doubt said, 'Well bowled' and, to the batsman, 'Well played'. It is unlikely, though, that Lord's allowed itself much more than a ripple of handclaps at the moment of dismissal – though there would be louder applause as Hobbs approached the pavilion. No batsman ever wants to be out; but there are some slight compensations. Even those accustomed to the experience will say that the applause of the Lord's pavilion had always a particularly warming effect. So it must have seemed to Greg Chappell when he came in at Lord's after scoring 131 – his first Test century in England – in the second match of the 1972 series. Going to bat when Australia were seven for two wickets, he had played the decisive, and by far the highest score of the match – over twice as many as any other individual innings – and set Australia on the course to winning a Test which they had entered one down with four to play in the rubber. In the event it was known as 'Massie's match' because the twenty-five-year-old seam bowler, Bob Massie, playing in his first Test, took sixteen wickets for 137 runs in a phenomenal display of swing bowling in helpful conditions. Chappell's innings, however, was one of stylish certainty. Tall and slim, he moved with the unhurried ease of the great batsman; he was, indeed, considered the finest on-side player of his time. Few cricketers ever receive the accolade of a standing ovation at Lord's, when, as the batsman approaches the pavilion, by a strange unanimity of recognition, and with no suggestion of pre-arrangement, the whole company of the members rise to their feet with a rustling noise like the passing of a great flock of birds, and the clapping gradually mounts to a crescendo. It is said that the hardest-headed Australian has a quasi-religious respect for Lord's, and feels an extra urge to succeed there. Such a salute is deeply moving, even to the ordinary observer; for the recipient, it must be a highly emotional experience.

Tony Greig came tantalisingly near to the same salute in his first Test as captain of England – against Australia at Lord's in 1975 – when he was out for 96. It is one of the many injustices of cricket – cruellest of games – that so vast a difference should be felt between a century and the narrowest non-century. Greig had won

Greg Chappell,
Lord's, 1972.

Greig, out for 96,
England v.
Australia, Lord's,
1975.

the toss and given England first innings on a good pitch. Lillee, though, took the first four wickets for 33 runs in ten overs: and Greig came in to join David Steele – who was playing in his first Test – at a precarious 49 for four. They put on 96 together for the fifth wicket and Greig went on strongly to make a further 77 with Knott for the sixth. Then, when Chappell rested Thomson and brought on Walker, Greig – at this reduction of pace if not of pressure – attempted a forcing, back-foot stroke, square on the off side. A combative extrovert, Greig had the reputation of rising to a challenge. Certainly he often seemed stimulated by the great occasion. He had reached 96, and there was no reason why he could not have come to his century in singles – or at least in safety – when he essayed that stroke, to do it with a four. He made contact too far from his body, edged, and was caught at slip. In that anguished expression there must be, surely, as well as disappointment, an element of self-disgust as he recognised the unnecessary and ruinous risk he had taken. In the same match, the Australian, Ross Edwards, having rendered his side similar recovery service, was out – LBW to Woolmer – for 99.

Quite apart from his outstanding ability as a wicketkeeper, Alan Knott has always been a highly competitive batsman, especially at Test level. In the Centenary Test at Melbourne in 1977, after Randall had played his remarkable innings of 174 and, with Amiss and Greig, led England within sight of a win, Knott buckled down to fighting the issue down to the end. He had mustered 25

Knott falls to Lillee,
Centenary Test,
Melbourne, 1977.

Lloyd, also
dismissed Lillee,
Sydney, 1975.

Randall out to
Hogg, Melbourne,
1978.

with Underwood for the ninth wicket, then seven with Willis; and England wanted only another 46 to win when he was LBW to Lillee who, with eleven wickets for 165, effectively won the match for Australia. Because he sometimes teased bowlers, some may have thought Knott a light-hearted cricketer; but all a dedicated player's concentration and determination are summed up in his mixture of frustration and disbelief as he realises, even before the umpire's signal, that it is all over. On the Australian faces there is both pleasure and relief at winning a match which, briefly, Randall had threatened to wrest from them.

The two aspects of a dismissal are apparent again as David Lloyd walks away from the wicket in the fifth – Sydney – Test of 1974-5. This was the six-Test series dominated by Thomson and Lillee, who emerged from it as one of the historic fast bowling pairs. Although Thomson, actually, and Lillee, virtually, played in only five matches each, they took 58 wickets between them: and England won only the game in which Thomson was absent and Lillee so injured that he bowled only six overs. Lloyd was one of a series of English batsmen battered and hustled out of

Test cricket by this aggressive pair. Here he has been caught by Thomson off Lillee and the pair join with Marsh (placed by his glove, around Thomson's waist) in mutual congratulation.

Overnight in 1978, Rodney Hogg became both a popular idol and a symbol to an Australian cricket public desperately in need of such a figure in defeat and faced with the threat of Packer. 'Hoggy, Hoggy, Hoggy,' the crowds chanted: he – and they – loved it. The entire Australian team's delight when Hogg had Randall LBW in England's second innings of the third Test of 1978-9, at Melbourne, was not merely a matter of personal congratulation. It seemed to be – and proved – the conclusive stroke in the win which put Australia back into contention for the rubber. Hogg – decisively – took 10 for 66. By the fifth Test he had beaten Arthur Mailey's fifty-eight-year old record of 36 wickets in a series against England; by the end of the six-match rubber he had raised the figure to 41.

At Edgbaston in 1975, Mike Denness captained England for the last time. The tide of luck had already set against him in Australia during the previous winter.

An early break-
through in the first
Test, Edgbaston,
1975.

Now he put Australia in to bat and, almost predictably, after they had scored 359, a thunderstorm gave their bowlers a pitch on which they put out England for 101 and 173 to win by an innings. In the first innings only Edrich (seventh out, for 34 in nearly three hours) held out against the pace attack of Lillee and Walker (Thomson had an off day). Greig was fifth out at 54, caught by Marsh off Walker in a scene typical of the outcricket of Ian Chappell's Australians during the dominance of Lillee, Thomson and Walker. (*See the photograph on pp. 2-3 of the book.*) The close catching of the side was outstanding and Marsh, for all his shambling, heavy-going approach, had come far from the stage when he was mockingly called 'iron gloves' to a safe-handed certainty. The flow of a cricket match can usually be sensed; when, at the start of the second English innings, Marsh caught Edrich off Walker, the fielding side converged on the wicketkeeper in an aggressive posse to congratulate him and parade their confidence.

Davis c. Knott b. Greig, Centenary Test, 1977.

Tony Greig has always been an extrovert; outwardly, at least, bursting with that brash apparent confidence which, the psychologists assure us, merely masks uncertainty. However that may be, no one would deny his flair for the theatrical. After two relatively even first innings (138 and 95) in the Centenary Test, Australia were 53 for three in their second when Ian Davis gave them – as it proved – a decisive stiffening with a sound if unspectacular 68 – until then the highest score on either side. When Greig had him caught at the wicket, though, it seemed that England still had the chance to win. Greig obviously thought so, and signalled his belief.

The 1978 West Indies–Australia series was bitterly unsatisfactory from the start. The Packer split, allegations of bad umpiring, and the rioting which prevented a finish when the final Test was going Australia's way, all combined to bedevil the rubber. In the course of Thomson's great burst in the second Test, at Bridgetown,

27

Greenidge is given
not out, West
Indies v. Australia,
Barbados, 1978.

Barbados, a lifting ball seemed to brush Gordon Greenidge's glove and the
Australian field – with a single exception – 'went up' for a catch at the wicket. Only
the elder of the chapel, Bobby Simpson, observed – or sensed – that the umpire was
not going to grant the appeal; and, surely enough, Greenidge was given not out.

It is sometimes argued that in modern Test cricket played, as a rule, on true,
easy batting wickets, matches tend early to take a set course. Still, from time to
time, some dramatic reversal of the trend recalls the game's classic uncertainty.
Indeed, some of the most successful strategies of modern times have been those of

captains who set out to take a grip on a match, doggedly denying stronger opponents clear advantage until they goaded them into taking a risk too many, giving an opening, and being beaten. Sometimes, though, the unforeseen happens, so rapidly and violently as to recall that, despite modern skills, caution, and defensive tactics, cricket remains the most unpredictable of games.

After the first two matches of their 1972-3 series with Australia had been drawn, West Indies needed 334 to win the third, played on a slow turning wicket at Port-of-Spain. Gibbs – above all – Inshan Ali and Willett should have given West Indies a clear advantage over a side whose spinners were Jenner, O'Keeffe and Stackpole. Fredericks made a conscientious 76; Murray, Kanhai and Lloyd destroyed themselves but, by lunch on the last day, Kallicharran and Foster had carried them to 268 for four: they needed only another 66 runs to win. Walker opened the bowling in the afternoon to Kallicharran, whose responsible innings of 91 deserved a century; but he pushed out surprisingly casually to the first ball of the afternoon and was caught at the wicket; Marsh again took the chance. O'Keeffe and Walker polished off the innings; the last six wickets fell for 21 and Australia won the key match of the rubber by 46 runs. The West Indian tail, certainly, was not strong; but it is difficult to avoid the conclusion that this was another of their temperamental losses of purpose. It had happened before: three times over entire series – to their strong team in England in 1957; in Australia, first in 1951-2 when they should have squared the series at two each, and then in 1975-6 when, after their spectacular innings win at Perth, they simply disintegrated. Equally, the Australians, throughout cricket history, have been quick to strike back even from a position of apparently imminent defeat.

Kallicharran c. Marsh b. Walker, Port of Spain, Trinidad, 1973.

Michael Holding

Michael Holding, the Jamaican, is one of the fastest bowlers in the history of cricket. Yet, up to the end of the 1975 season in West Indies, when he was 22, he had the indifferent record of 16 wickets (at 51 runs apiece) in three domestic seasons, and had never played in a Test. Indeed, for a time he almost gave up cricket in favour of athletics. As it was, picked as partner for Roberts in Australia in 1975-6, he took four wickets in the second Test, which West Indies won. Then he was injured, and did not fully recover on that tour. He went back, though, to a home series against India when he took nineteen wickets – and was criticised for too often pitching short – in the four Tests before he came to England in 1976.

There he rose to a high peak of ability. With a sprinter's approach to the wicket – umpires often looked round to make sure he was coming up to bowl because his footfalls were so light that they did not hear him – he bowled from a high action with the whip-through of a lithe physique. Not fit to play in the first Test, he took three wickets in the second; seven in the third, when he was warned for intimidation; four in the fourth. The Oval pitch for the fifth Test was as deadly slow as had been expected. The other fast or fast medium bowlers in the match – Roberts, Holder, Daniel, King, Willis, Selvey (Greig bowled largely off breaks) – took six wickets between them. Holding, bowling very straight and to a fairly full length –

using the bouncer only occasionally, to unsettle a batsman – took 14 wickets, more than any West Indian bowler in a Test before, for 149. It is significant that, in the entire match, 28 wickets fell for 1507 runs; an average of 53.8 runs each; Holder's personal figure was 10.64. Even more amazingly, the 28 wickets fell within 423 overs – or one in every fifteen – while Holding's striking rate was one every four. It is difficult to believe that there has ever been a comparable sustained spell of accurate and penetrative fast bowling on a slow wicket: some might question if there has ever been quite so fast a spell.

A thoughtful, and mildly mannered young man, and a computer programmer employed by the Jamaican government, Holding was, rarely among West Indian cricketers, not wildly anxious for a professional career, though some tempting offers were made after that performance at The Oval. It seems probable that he joined the Packer operation as one of a team.

Some indication of Holding's speed – and line – can be gathered from the fact that, of his fourteen wickets, nine were bowled and three were LBW.

To view his victims in order, Balderstone touched a yorker on its way to the stumps (few people can have had a more savage entry into Test cricket than Balderstone's two matches against the Roberts, Holding, Daniel, Holder and King battery).

Balderstone, out for 0.

The victims,
Greig, Underwood,
Amiss, Knott . . .

Greig was yorked through a startled jump. That prompted a pitch invasion by West Indians who had not forgotten – and did not allow Greig to forget – his promise to make them 'grovel'.

Underwood covered his off stump after it was gone.

Amiss, even after he had scored 203, was simply beaten for pace and bowled behind his legs by a ball that brushed his pad.

Knott, after a game fifty, was bowled off the inside edge of a back stroke.

Selvey was dismissed first ball, again comprehensively bowled.

Selvey,
Balderstone, Greig
and Knott.

In the second innings, Balderstone did not manage to touch his yorker and completed a 'pair'.

To the delight of the West Indians, Greig was yorked, leg stump, by his first ball from Holding. All opponents, regardless of country or county, seem to have felt an extra satisfaction at taking Tony Greig's wicket; the West Indies were no exception.

Knott played another brave innings; this time of 57, before he received one of the best balls of this – or any other – season, a blind length break-back, pitching just outside the off stump and hoisting the middle stump out of the ground.

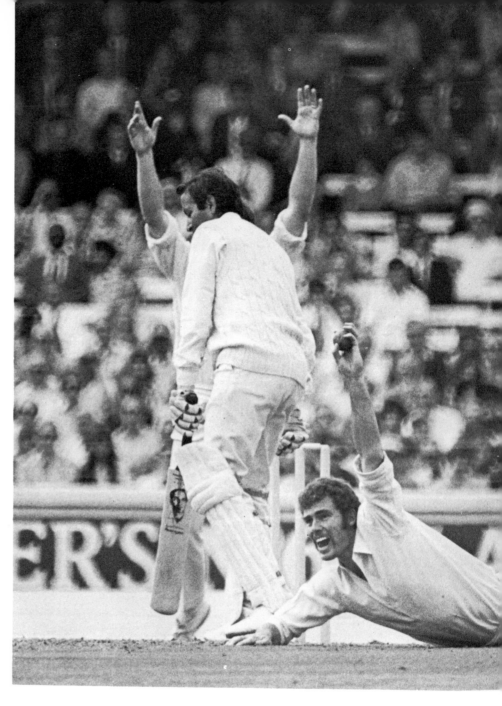

'Catch It'

Anyone who frequents cricketing circles knows only too well the eternal plaint that something – batting, bowling, umpiring, sportsmanship, or whatever – 'is not what is used to be'. No one, though, will deny that fielding – including placing and, especially, close catching – is not only incomparably better than it was even twenty years ago but possibly, as it seemed in Australia in 1978-9, growing even finer.

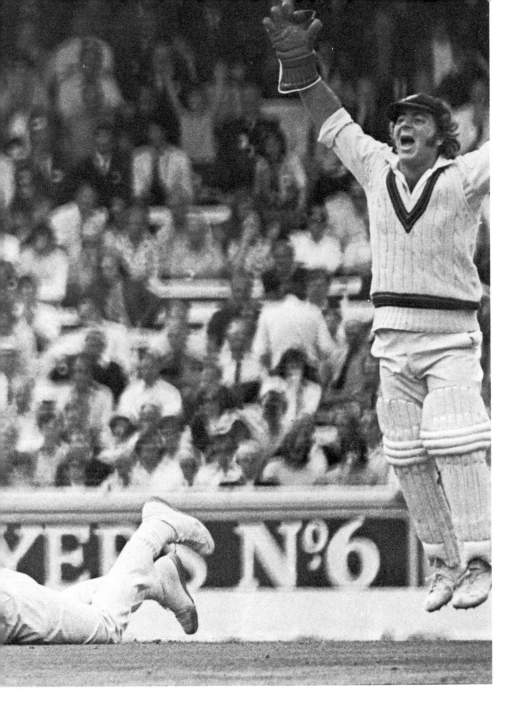

D'Oliveira c. Greg Chappell b. Mallett, England v. Australia, fifth Test, The Oval, 1972.

The key to this improvement undoubtedly lies in concentration; the captains who lifted the standard insisted on unrelenting attention: close fieldsmen do not talk in the moments up to and including action (except sometimes as a psychological ploy, to unsettle a batsman). In this tense silence spectators can often hear, in the split second as a ball leaves the bat edge or – for the avoidance of doubt in a case of bat-pad – two or three of the close field shout 'catch it!'

Australia twice came from behind to square the rubber of 1972. Their win in the fifth Test at The Oval drew the series; but England, the holders, retained The Ashes. That match still provides the only instance of brothers – Ian and Greg

Botham, in crash helmet, catches Edgar off Edmonds, England v. New Zealand, second Test, Trent Bridge, 1978.

Chappell – scoring centuries in the same Test innings. Greg, a capable fieldsman anywhere, had the satisfaction, too, of taking a difficult catch when he threw himself forward in Mallett's leg trap to put out D'Oliveira. For D'Oliveira it was a sad moment; this proved his last Test innings.

The high standard of English close fielding under Mike Brearley was emphasised against New Zealand in 1978. Brearley's fortune lay in the fact that so many of the men worth their places as batsmen or bowlers were also outstanding catchers. One such was Ian Botham who ended the suspense for his captain, Bob Taylor – and Bruce Edgar – when he held up the catch off the left-handed New Zealand

opening batsman; Edmonds was the bowler. Botham himself said that he felt he might have flinched momentarily and, possibly, have dropped it if he had not been wearing a helmet.

Ian Chappell was the first Australian to take a hundred catches in Test cricket. A combative player, a strictly pragmatic batsman, and a hostile and astute captain, he was also an outstanding fieldsman. He set his record when he caught Lawrence Rowe off Thomson – a stinger in his specialist slip position – at Melbourne in 1975-6.

The Centenary Test was, simply, a success; weather, event, bowling, batting,

Rowe c. Ian
Chappell b.
Thomson,
Australia v. West
Indies, third Test,
Melbourne, 1975-6.

fielding, company, all went well. There was a whole crop of good catches. As England pressed on the collapsing Australian first innings, Old constantly bowled 'through the gate' at the left-handed Gilmour; finally he made one leave him and Greig, taking off to his right from second slip, held the catch and was in mid-air when he passed Brearley at first slip. For a man of his height and length of arm, Greig has always been surprisingly coherent physically and a most capable catcher.

That made Australia 117 for eight; but Greg Chappell was still in and batting calmly; and O'Keeffe, who joined him, is a capable, orthodox batsman with a sound defence. To keep the game tight, Greig brought up Underwood, who made one go with his arm; O'Keeffe, playing for the turn, got a top edge; the ball spun up over his and Knott's heads and Brearley, going a long way to his left from first slip, made the catch behind the wicketkeeper. Brearley's naturally quick reactions, his determination, concentration and 'clean' hands combine to make him a highly capable slip – which has in turn enabled him to demand, and deploy, a high standard of fielding in his England team.

O'Keeffe c. Brearley b. Underwood, Centenary Test, Melbourne, 1977.

Gilmour c. Greig b. Old, Centenary Test, Melbourne, 1977.

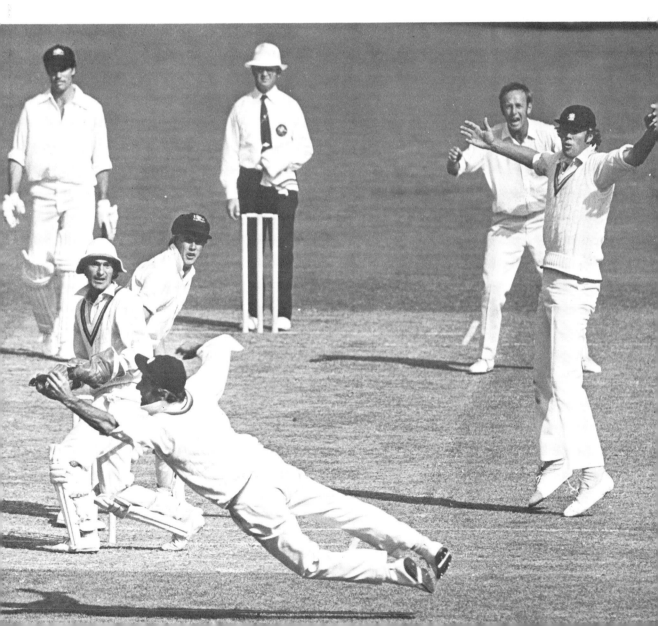

McCosker c. Knott
b. Greig, England v.
Australia, fourth
Test, Headingley,
1977.

Over the period of a decade, and in 89 Test matches, Alan Knott set a record for the number of dismissals by a wicketkeeper in Test cricket of 252 (233 caught and 19 stumped), 33 more than anyone else has achieved in Test cricket; though the Australian Bertie Oldfield made 52 stumpings in his 54 matches. For a relatively short man, Knott, vibrantly restless, reached some extremely difficult chances. At Headingley, in 1977, McCosker's edge off Greig would have fallen short of Brearley at first slip but Knott went a very long way to scoop up the catch.

In Melbourne, during the 1974-5 tour, Knott's Australian contemporary, Rodney Marsh, caught him off Thomson, landing almost as wide as a wide first slip; eyes on the ball until it was in the gloves. Marsh has made 190 catches and

Knott c. Marsh b.
Thomson, England
v. Australia, third
Test, Melbourne,
1974-5.

eight stumpings in 52 matches; an extremely high striking rate. For all his heavy build, short legs and shambling approach, he is highly mobile.

After the Australian tour to South Africa planned for 1975-6 had been cancelled, West Indies agreed to go to Australia two years earlier than scheduled. Clive Lloyd won the toss in the first Test, at Brisbane, and his batsmen embarked upon a prodigal morning's play. In two hours, eighteen overs were bowled, 125 runs were scored by utterly carefree stroke-play, and six wickets fell. Vivian Richards, in one of his rare Test failures, flicked at Lillee and Gilmour, at fourth slip, took the catch splendidly in his 'wrong' hand after it seemed to have passed him. That was Dennis Lillee's hundredth Test wicket.

OVERLEAF:
Richards c.
Gilmour b. Lillee,
Australia v. West
Indies, first Test,
Brisbane, 1975-6.

Walker c. Lloyd b.
Roberts, Australia
v. West Indies,
fourth Test,
Sydney, 1975-6.

Boycott is dropped by McCosker, England v. Australia, third Test, Trent Bridge, 1977.

In the fourth – Sydney – Test of that rubber, Greg Chappell, dropped at slip by Boyce off Roberts when he had made 11, went on to score 182 not out. Next day Roberts came back to destroy the Australian tail. Walker snicked him and the ball was still rising when Clive Lloyd – a great fieldsman anywhere – caught it virtually through the fingers of the leaping Vivian Richards.

Just lest this sequence should seem a chronicle of infallibility, let us see some of the catches that were, as the Australians say, 'spilt'. Bhagwat Chandrasekhar has been a match-winning bowler for India. Despite a right arm impaired by polio-myelitis he bowls leg breaks, top spinners and googlies at a surprisingly brisk speed through the air and with unexpected pace off the wicket. His spin is not great but, given a little help and life from the pitch, he 'does' enough to go 'through' the stroke, especially of a batsman who attempts to play him off the back foot. Even when as quick-footed a batsman as Roger Tolchard moved forward to him in Calcutta in 1977, Chandra found the edge, but the ball flew so high and wide that Kirmani's desperate effort achieved no more than a finger-tip touch.

Kirmani drops Tolchard off Chandra, India v. England, second Test, Calcutta, 1976-7.

In 1977 Geoffrey Boycott returned to international cricket at Trent Bridge after a voluntary exile of 30 Tests. In the face of Australia's first innings of 243, England were 82 for five, and Boycott had batted three hours for 20 when he edged Len Pascoe. As slip catches go – and they are never simple – this was a straightforward chance to McCosker, who dropped it. Boycott had made 107 before McCosker eventually caught him off Thomson. Boycott scored 80 not out in the second innings as England won by seven wickets, and he ended the series with a record average of 147.33.

Almost exactly a year later, and also at Trent Bridge, Boycott, having missed all three matches against Pakistan and the first against New Zealand, made yet another return to Test cricket for the second match with New Zealand. At the outset of his innings, Richard Hadlee, bowling faster and better than at any other time on the tour, harrassed and disturbed him. In his third over he fired a break-back through Boycott's hesitant stroke and had a reasonable 'shout'; then he found the edge, only for Geoffrey Howarth to drop an extremely awkward chance at third slip. There was to be no further chance and, just before six o'clock, after almost five-and-a-half hours of determined, patient batting, Boycott reached yet another Test century – and was still there at the end of the day, 108 not out.

Eagerness can trap even the best of players into error. In the Headingley Test of 1976, Snow wanted one wicket for two hundred in Tests; Knott one dismissal to pass Godfrey Evans' Test record of 219. Wayne Daniel, by no means a distinguished bat, snicked Snow, and Knott, diving anxiously in front of the slips, dropped the chance. Almost immediately Snow bowled Roberts to reach his objective; and, later, when England batted, capably held the opposite end while

Boycott is again dropped – this time by Howarth off Hadlee, England v. New Zealand, second Test, Trent Bridge, 1978.

Knott drops Daniel off Snow, England v. West Indies, fourth Test, Headingley, 1976.

Knott reached his century. Knott, though, had an unusually barren second innings in the field, and had to wait a fortnight before he broke the record, which he finally achieved at The Oval.

These, though, are the rare aberrations of normally safe, expert catchers. This is in many ways a most important branch of the current game, in that it is the section most likely to show improvement. To bat, bowl or keep wicket to a consistently successful standard at Test level demands something akin to genius. It has been proved, though, that men with quick reactions can be made into match-winning – and 'match-winning' is the significant term – fieldsmen by fitness and aptitude training, concentration and the motivation of a good captain. That was proved the first time a captain ordered a slothful mid-on to move off his heels on to his toes and to move forward as the bowler came in to bowl. Jack Hobbs turned himself from an indifferent fielder, usually employed at third man, to one of the finest cover points the game has known; and many other players – notably Geoffrey Boycott – have improved their fielding almost beyond recognition. In short, fielding is the one department of the game where, by taking thought – and practice – a man may effectively add a cubit to his stature, and increase the effectiveness of his team.

By the Skin of the Teeth

Some of the deepest agonies, most tragic – and most comic – muddles, most grotesque losses of equilibrium and dignity, and most difficult umpiring decisions are produced by – or produce – run outs. There is a technique, a series of safeguards which should protect a batsman; but no one has ever gone unscathed. Jack Hobbs probably was the greatest of all runners between wickets. In partnership with Wilfred Rhodes, Herbert Sutcliffe and Andrew Sandham, he took hundreds of runs which would not have been apparent to the average player. 'We got to know each other so well,' he said of his three partners, 'that we hardly needed to call; and I think I only ever had one run out with Wilfred – and that was

Hampshire v. Kent, Southampton, 1974: Asif Ibqual is the batsman, Bob Stephenson the 'keeper

when he slipped – and one with Herbert.' Sir Jack also had a considerable record on the other side: he is said to have run out sixteen opponents on the 1907-8 tour of Australia.

Others have proved more fallible. Some simply are not good runners; the Australian Graeme Wood had a tragic series against England in 1978-9; and Walter Robins once said of Denis Compton, 'If he calls you for a run, regard it as no more than a basis for negotiation.'

Run outs probably present umpires with more problems even than LBW decisions especially since, when an umpire is at the bowler's end, he often does not have time to take up a balanced position to judge line and batsman. But a pair of photographs taken during the Hampshire v. Kent match at Southampton in 1974 shows that Bob Stephenson took a return from the field and comfortably ran

51

Hampshire v.
Pakistan,
Portsmouth, 1971.
Richard Gilliat is
the batsman,
Wasim Bari the
'keeper

out Asif Iqbal. At least one spectator saluted the performance – yet the umpire ruled Asif not out.

The direct throw to hit the stumps is always spectacular while, for the batsman, it invariably comes as a shock. Jack Hobbs, Gilbert Jessop, Cyril Washbrook, Gul Mahommad, Clive Lloyd and, even in a short career, David Gower, have all made reputations for the direct hit. In the Pakistanis' match with Hampshire at Portsmouth in 1971, Zaheer Abbas, from cover point, exploded Richard Gilliat's off stump out of the ground ahead of his run.

In the course of Boycott's century on his return to Test cricket in 1977 at Trent Bridge, he ran out Derek Randall in the kind of tragic muddle that the efficiency of modern fielding infallibly punishes. Taking Thomson's return, Marsh happily demolished the wicket. No one who runs out Randall at Trent Bridge should expect to be popular; and office staff in the neighbouring block hung recriminatory posters in their windows – increasing the onus at least upon Boycott to make a century; the crowd saluted him, in partial forgiveness, when he did so.

Randall is run out,
England v.
Australia, third
Test, Trent Bridge,
1977.

The final of the 1975 Prudential World Cup – West Indies v. Australia – was, beyond question, decided by the five run outs in the Australian innings. The first three – of Turner and the two Chappells – which brought Australia down to 162 for four, were all the work of Vivian Richards, with two direct throws and a return to the bowler. The second of those two, a throw on the run from short midwicket, accounted for Alan Turner.

Vivian Richards
runs out Alan
Turner, Prudential
Cup Final, West
Indies v. Australia,
Lord's, 1975.

The Big Hit

The big hit – for six – is the most companionable of cricketing acts. Casting the unfortunate bowler in the part of clown, it infallibly puts the crowds in a satisfied, laughing mood. Six sixes, such as those struck by Sobers off Nash in a single over at Swansea – and since shown on television so often that some must think he never did anything else – made a positive feast of entertainment.

The six hit is, officially, a relatively new definition. Originally all hits were run out. Nyren tells how in matches at Hambledon, played, of course, on the high downland, the fair-minded crowd used to open to give fieldsmen of opposing teams unhampered passage to pursue the ball 'to the feet of the surrounding mountains'. By about the 1880s almost all grounds marked a boundary line and any ball which crossed it counted four. It was still only four though, if it passed over the boundary in the air. It has often been argued that, under the present law, England would have won the Old Trafford Test of 1902 which, in the event, they lost by three runs – and the rubber with it. At that time a six was awarded only for a ball hit out of the ground. Even Albert Trott's famous hit – of 1899 – over the top of the Lord's pavilion, only counted four.

It was not until 1910 that it was officially 'recommended' – no more – that six be awarded for a stroke where the ball cleared the boundary before pitching. Even the boundary is not defined, but falls within the 'how long is a piece of string' category. The laws specify that: 'In deciding on the allowances to be made for boundaries the umpires will be guided by the prevailing custom of the ground.' In 1957, in the interest of increasing the game's spectator attraction rather than of uniformity, it was decided that in first-class cricket the boundary should be set 75 yards from the wicket, and that practice has, in general, been continued; but it is not mandatory.

The more calculating cricketers usually consider that six hitting is 'not business'. Essex, during Trevor Bailey's captaincy, made calculations based on their own and opponents' play and concluded that, among batsmen prepared to hit fairly judiciously, the average ration was three sixes before a good county bowler took his wicket, probably caught in the deep field.

Still there are those players who will go for the big hit, especially the natural – perhaps compulsive is the word – hookers. It is not fortuitous that only one of the hitters in these pictures is English.

The classic instance of the six that wasn't comes from the first Prudential World Cup final. Ian Chappell won the toss, put West Indies in to bat and Fredericks and Greenidge settled almost at once into an apparently comfortable form. When Lillee dropped short, Roy Fredericks, a volatile, wiry left-hander, hooked him violently and high to long leg with a stroke so violent that it flung him off his feet. In falling, he hit the stumps with a foot, dislodging the bails, and was given out hit wicket. Meanwhile, the nearby Australian fieldsman, Doug Walters, was contemplating the 'six'.

Fredericks' partner that day, Gordon Greenidge, is one of the most powerful strikers of the ball in modern cricket: a batsman of basically correct method but immense and joyous enthusiasm and considerable strength. In 1976 he had a fine run of success against England. In the course of his 84 in the first innings at Lord's, he hooked a short ball from Snow so heartily as to swing himself off his feet and to bring a brief smile of approval to Brian Close's face.

Greenidge followed with three centuries in successive Test innings and then,

RIGHT: Gordon Greenidge drives Willis for six, England v. West Indies, fifth Test, The Oval, 1976.

56

Fredericks hooks
Lillee for what
would have been a
six, but . . .
Prudential Cup
Final, Lord's, 1975.

58

Greenidge hooks Snow for six, England v. West Indies, second Test, Lords, 1976.

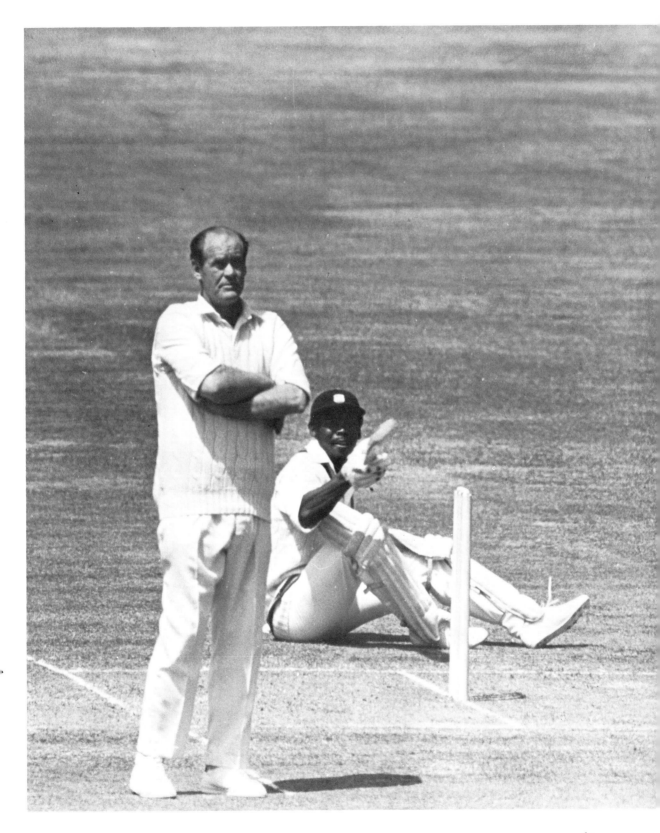

after making nought in the first innings at The Oval, when Lloyd called for quick runs in the second against a declaration he scored 85 in 140 minutes. In the course of that innings he drove an only slightly overpitched ball from Willis – bowling at considerable pace – almost straight for a six of savagely clean power.

At Perth in the 1974-5 series Doug Walters – the prolific Australian stroke-maker who has never showed his best form in England – went in just before tea on the second day. As Willis came up to bowl the final ball of the day, Walters' score was 97. The entire crowd realised that he needed three for his century; but few of them remembered that, three not out at tea, he wanted a six to have scored a hundred in the session. Walters – always an intriguing mixture of shrewdness and naïveté – knew well enough. Willis dropped short and Walters hooked him – not fine, not square but, in his confident impatience, to midwicket – for six and, hardly waiting to see it land, walked briskly away.

David Gower, of Leicestershire, emerged in 1978 as the best young batsman in England. A stylish left-hander with an easy confidence, he never feared to play strokes and at The Oval, in the first New Zealand Test of that summer, he drove Boock – slow left arm – straight for a long six. There was no possible doubt about it, never any hint of the need to run; all present could stand and watch the ball drop far beyond the boundary, into the pavilion seats.

RIGHT: Gower
drives Boock for
six, England v. New
Zealand, first Test,
the Oval, 1978.

Richards during his innings of 102, Hampshire v. Middlesex, John Player League, Lord's, 1977.

Barry Richards, the South African who played for Hampshire, was, arguably, the most gifted batsman of his generation. He is a splendidly versatile stroke-maker, but his country's racial doctrines have restricted his Test career to a single, quite successful series. However, he faced all the best bowlers of his time with consistently outstanding results. His team-mates believed he could 'turn it on' as and when he wished. There is evidence that bears this out. When his parents came over to see him in 1976 he greeted their arrival with a century on the Saturday of the Whit weekend match against Kent. That evening, at dinner, his father congratulated him and jokingly commented that it would have been more appropriate on the Tuesday, which was his mother's birthday. 'She shall have one,' said Richards and, surely enough, made 108 in less than an hour-and-a-half. It has been said, too, that he was inspired by the television cameras. Certainly, in the televised John Player League match between Hampshire and Middlesex at Lord's in 1977 he effectively won the match with an innings of 102 in which he hit four sixes; one of which brought him his fifty and the other – photographed here – his century.

The Human Target

The physical element – the impact of the ball on the batsman's body – is as old as cricket. In the underarm days of Hambledon, Nyren could write of David Harris's deliveries: 'Woe be to the man who did not get in to block them, for they had such a peculiar curl that they would grind his fingers against the bat: many a time have I seen the blood drawn in this way from a batter who was not up to the trick.'

In the first Test match, at Melbourne in 1877, the Yorkshireman, 'Happy Jack' Ulyett, assailed the Australian opening batsmen, Charles Bannerman – who scored a century – with a series of short-pitched balls, one of which broke Bannerman's finger and forced him to retire hurt (for 165 in a total of 245). Generally, in the past, fast bowlers were content to employ the short-pitched ball as, in Frank Tyson's term, 'a reminder' – a warning to the batsman that he could not rely upon so full a length that he could step up to drive. Undoubtedly, however, Gregory and McDonald in 1921, Larwood and Voce in 1932-3, and Lindwall and Miller in the 1946-53 period, regularly used the bouncer as a tactical weapon; though, except in the case of the 1932-3 'Bodyline', it was usually employed for its surprise or intimidation value. Since the nineteen-seventies the proportion of bouncers has steadily increased; partly as intimidation, but equally for the tactical reason that many of the best batsmen will attempt to hook the hookable ball, and, for most, that is not a controllable stroke, and they are liable to lift it. Some hook compulsively; indeed, Frank Tyson entitled his book on the 1975-6 Australia–West Indies series *The Hapless Hookers*. Some players, notably Bobby Simpson, have conditioned themselves to the fact that the hook is in the long run unprofitable, and play no stroke to the short-pitched ball. Simpson simply kept his eye on the rising ball and swayed inside or outside it so safely that bowlers eventually realised they were wasting their time in directing bouncers at him.

The bouncer is a violent ball; but it would be wrong to believe that it is used solely with violent intent.

Bowlers and captains persist with it because, year in, year out, it is an effective weapon against the best players. Why is it effective? In the first place because it is fast. A bouncer delivered at anything below truly high pace – even fast medium – is simply a long hop, a free hit to any capable batsman. Secondly, because its height makes it almost impossible for the batsman to get over it, it compels a virtually uncontrollable stroke: whether the hook or a defensive parry, it is likely to produce a catch. Sir Donald Bradman eventually became a highly capable hooker – perhaps the best there has been – because he got over the ball and kept it down with a roll of the wrists; if he could not get over it, he would not play a hook. Genuinely fast bowling, too, finds out batsmen short of the highest class because their reactions are not quick enough to deal with it. That is not a matter of courage or the lack of it; simply the speed of the reflexes. There is, too, the question of physical danger; and that applies to every man. No one relishes the impact – or the possibility of the impact – of a cricket ball travelling at ninety miles an hour. As Morris Leyland, put it, 'None on us likes it, but some shows it more than others.' It has been observed, too, that a series of blows will reduce a batman's confidence and concentration. During the Bodyline series, while most of the major Australian batsmen scored a century, none made a second after taking a physical beating.

RIGHT: Iqbal Qasim is hit by Willis, England v. Pakistan, first Test, Edgbaston, 1978.

Crucially, from the tactical point of view, the knowledge that the bowler can and probably will bowl a bouncer induces the batsman to be in two minds. In the shortest possible time he must decide between a stroke which defends his wicket and one which defends his head. Since the two are totally different, the adjustment must be rapid; often rapid enough to result in a mistimed or mishit stroke.

For all these reasons it is unlikely that the bouncer will be renounced or forbidden. The only indication to the contrary lay in the uncontrolled intensification of the bouncer barrage in World Series – Packer – cricket, where the six or seven fastest bowlers in the world might be engaged in a single one-day match and the batsmen do not relish it. Otherwise, as a steadily increasing number of players have realised, however unattractive it may look, the crash helmet is the best practicable solution.

An important advance in limiting the use of the bouncer was the tentative note that it should not be used against non-batsmen. It was reinforced after an incident at Edgbaston in 1978 in the first Test between England and Pakistan. Iqbal Qasim was sent in as night watchman when Pakistan's first second innings wicket – Mudassar's – fell in the last over of the third day. Next morning, in that manner of tail-end batsmen which so infuriates bowlers, Iqbal Qasim hung on. He had scored five in 49 minutes when Willis, no doubt irritated, bowled a bouncer to him. Unfortunately he delivered it from round the wicket. Iqbal Qasim is quite short and, importantly, not an accomplished batsman. He made a desperate mess of an attempted defensive back stroke and was hit on the mouth. He retired hurt; hospital treatment consisted of two stitches in a wound in his lip, and he took no further part in the match. It was strongly felt that it was unethical to bowl such a ball to so poor a batsman. As a result it was decided that the captains should attempt to reach agreement on those batsmen who were incapable of dealing with short-pitched fast bowling, and to ensure that it was not used against them. The arrangement proved satisfactory.

At Melbourne in 1978-9, Rick Darling, the young Australian batsman, lost his balance and his helmet in attempting to play a lifting ball from Willis who, after his successes in the first and second Tests, had a poor time. Troubled by blistered toes, the England bowler took no wicket for 68 runs in the match.

At Port-of-Spain, in the first West Indies–Australia Test of 1977-8, Peter Toohey, the Australian batsman, was hit on the forehead when he tried to hook a lifter from Andy Roberts. In the event the injury proved to be less serious than it looked; but when Toohey resumed his innings he was hit on the hand and fractured a finger so seriously that he was forced to miss the two following Tests.

The Australian fast bowlers always made Keith Fletcher a target for the bouncer. At Sydney, in 1974-5, he tried to cover up to a ball from Thomson which flew off his glove, hit the English crest on his cap and rebounded so far to the off side that it was only a little short of a catch to Ross Edwards at cover.

Derek Underwood has always been a game – even enthusiastic – candidate for the post of night watchman; his enthusiasm was only temporarily dimmed when he was hit by a thrown bouncer from Charlie Griffith at Trent Bridge in 1966. Determinedly staying on line and, correct though hurried, he played a steeply rising ball from Sarfraz in the third – Oval – Test with Pakistan in 1974.

Underwood has always maintained that the way to deal with the bouncer is to play it; not to hook, duck or sway, but to play it. He was attempting to do that when one from Holding howled past him at Old Trafford in 1976.

Considering the extent of the bowling of bouncers, official warnings for

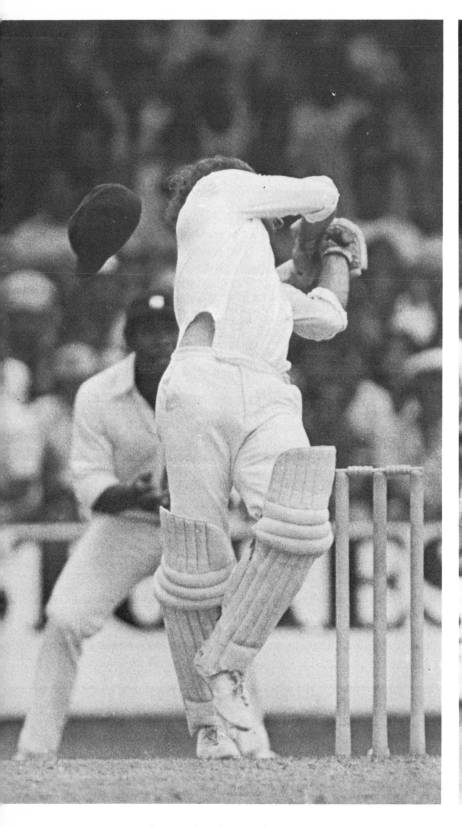

Toohey is hit by Roberts, West Indies v. Australia, first Test, Port-of-Spain, Trinidad, 1978.

Fletcher is hit by
Walker, Australia
v. England, fourth
Test, Sydney,
1974-5.

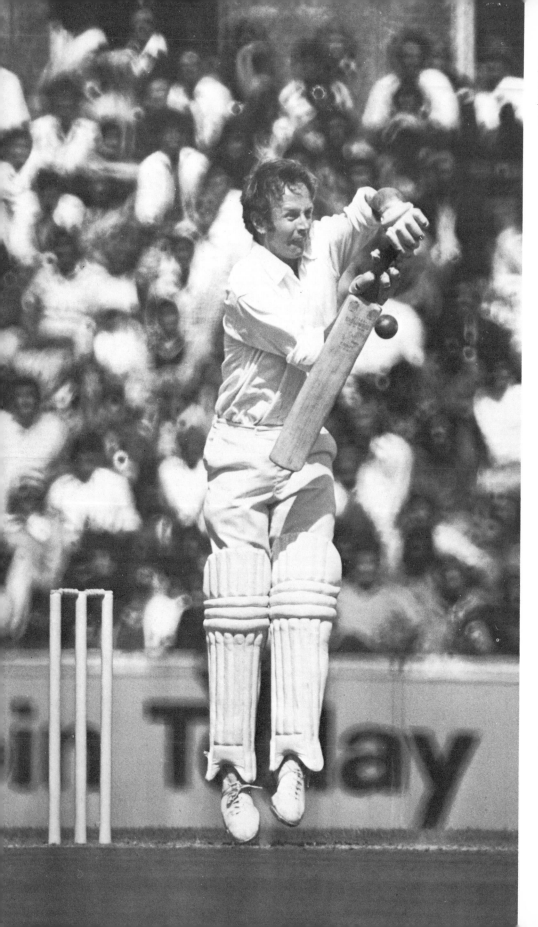

Underwood on his toes against Sarfraz, England v. Pakistan, third Test, the Oval, 1974.

Underwood
against Holding,
England v. West
Indies, third Test,
Old Trafford, 1976.

Holding is warned by umpire Bill Alley, England v. West Indies, third Test, Old Trafford, 1976.

excessive use of the tactic are extremely rare. Bill Alley, though, administered one to Michael Holding in the second English innings at Old Trafford in 1976. Both Greig and Underwood narrowly escaped injury in a frightening three-man (Holding, Roberts, Daniel) bombardment of short-pitched balls. Brian Close and John Edrich took a heavy beating and Clive Lloyd, the West Indian captain, admitted afterwards: 'Our fellows got carried away. They knew they only had eighty minutes that night and they went flat out, sacrificing accuracy for speed. They knew afterwards they had bowled badly.'

Alan Knott, a batsman of courage and determination, batted consistently bravely in the Australian series of 1974-5 when Thomson and Lillee routed England to take the rubber by four matches to one. Thomson could make Knott jump, but could not drive him off the line of the stumps. Knott finished third in the batting averages, second in aggregate (364 runs at 36.40) in those Tests, ahead of others with higher expectations as batsmen.

Knott against Thomson, Australia v. England, third Test, Melbourne, 1974.

Cowdrey is hit by Roberts, Kent v. Hampshire, Basingstoke, 1974.

In 1974 the West Indian, Andy Roberts, played his first full season of county cricket, for Hampshire, and finished top of the first class bowling averages with the remarkable figures of 119 wickets at a striking rate of one every six overs, and an average of 13.62. His previous experience of the first class game was slight but, thoughtful and intelligent, leanly strong and genuinely fast, he learnt and matured rapidly. Soon his new colleagues spoke with something near awe of his 'slow bouncer' and 'fast bouncer'. Colin Cowdrey was a victim of the artfully concealed difference in the Hampshire–Kent match at Basingstoke in that first season. At the start of his innings, Roberts bowled him the 'slow' bouncer which Cowdrey hooked firmly, though not particularly hard, and it was fielded. An over later came the 'fast' bouncer dropped on to the same spot. Cowdrey again shaped to hook, realised the extra pace of the ball and tried to pull away, but was too late. He was hit on the head and took no further part in the match. Hampshire won by an innings and 71 runs by tea on the second day and Roberts had match figures of nine for 39.

Brearley's arm is broken by Sikhander Bakht, a Sind XI v. England, Karachi, 1978.

Congdon is hit on the jaw by Snow, England v. New Zealand, first Test, Trent Bridge, 1973.

In the first – Trent Bridge – England–New Zealand Test of 1973, John Snow hit Bev Congdon on the jaw with a bouncer. So far from being disturbed by the blow, Congdon went steadily on to score 176; and followed it with 175 at Lord's.

Almost ironically, after these illustrations of such violent deliveries, the ball bowled by Sikhander Bakht on 15 January 1978 was of no more than his normal medium pace. It rose from a pitch of uneven bounce at Karachi where the match between Sind and the English touring side was played, and broke Mike Brearley's left forearm. He was flown back to England for an operation; a steel plate was inserted to support the fracture while it healed. He missed the third Test in Pakistan and the entire tour of New Zealand: Geoffrey Boycott took over the captaincy.

Impromptu play
and portable
refreshment are
available on a
Bombay Maidan
against a backdrop
as impressive as
any for cricket
anywhere in the
world.

Oddities and Quiddities

Because it is a game which runs the gamut between high speed action and
complete repose, violence and contemplation, humour and tragedy, cricket is full
of oddities and quiddities – ideas, distillates, vignettes, comicalities, peeps,
shocks, contrasts, harmonies and curiosities. Many of them happen and are lost in
a flicker of time, to be captured only by a photographer with a finger itching on the
shutter. The section that follows was extracted from an actual cardboard file but,
essentially, from a mental filing system which recorded eighteen years of items
not necessarily of interest to a news-conscious editor, or a history-seeking author,

but piquant, diverting, or simply pictorially appealing to the quizzical photographer.

All cricketers are cricketers, none the less so for not being 'first-class', which is no more than a statistical distinction. A bad batsman, bowler and fielder may not play in what is called first class cricket, yet be what his friends – and all real cricketers – would call first class as a cricketing man. Play extends far beyond the Test match grounds and the nearer it is to everyday life the more vivid and revealing its background.

The Bombay cricketers can use a Maidan, but not as a private cricket ground. Although matches and practice go on, the public of the city are still free to stroll there and the cow demonstrates its right of presence in Indian life and landscape.

OVERLEAF:
A Maidan,
Bombay.

Street scene, Karachi.

Cricket is now becoming as deeply rooted in the people of the Indian sub-continent as in the more spontaneous players of West Indies; or as football in the Mediterranean and South American countries. In this Karachi street match, the gestures are clearly inherited from the players' seniors. This dismissal will demand the use of a mallet to drive the stump back into the road surface.

The right-hand photograph shows the English game played in its Oriental setting; a permanent concrete pitch in Karachi.

86

ABOVE: Boys who live in the cane field area of Barbados are often hard put to find twenty-two-yards of true and level ground. For them, the only practicable pitch is the road; in this case, one in fairly frequent use by (invariably sympathetic) car drivers.

ABOVE RIGHT: The beach cricket of Barbados is a unique game. Played with a hard rubber ball, it generally involves mass fields – especially in the slips – many of them standing up to their thighs in water – short innings, and bowlers' mastery. The particular knack of the successful bowlers is to deliver when the retreating surf has left the shallowest possible film of water on the sand, from which the ball will rise steeply and unpredictably.

RIGHT: In Trinidad schoolgirls feel as entitled to use the practice ground for a stroll as the players for cricket.

FAR RIGHT: The vast expanse of Queen's Park, Savannah has room for thirty games of cricket to be played simultaneously.

The members of the West Indian under-nineteen touring side in England, 1978, must have found the setting of Southill Park, Bedfordshire, above – a splendid example of the country house ground – a cool contrast with their own sunny islands. They gave a good account of themselves there, though, and appreciated a wicket good enough to be used for Minor Counties matches. Swan Green, Lyndhurst, left, sets cricket in an idyllic New Forest glade only a few strides from a busy main road (a six can, and sometimes does, hit a passing motor car).

The Taylor twins, Benson and Hedges competition, Somerset v. Hampshire, Taunton, 1974.

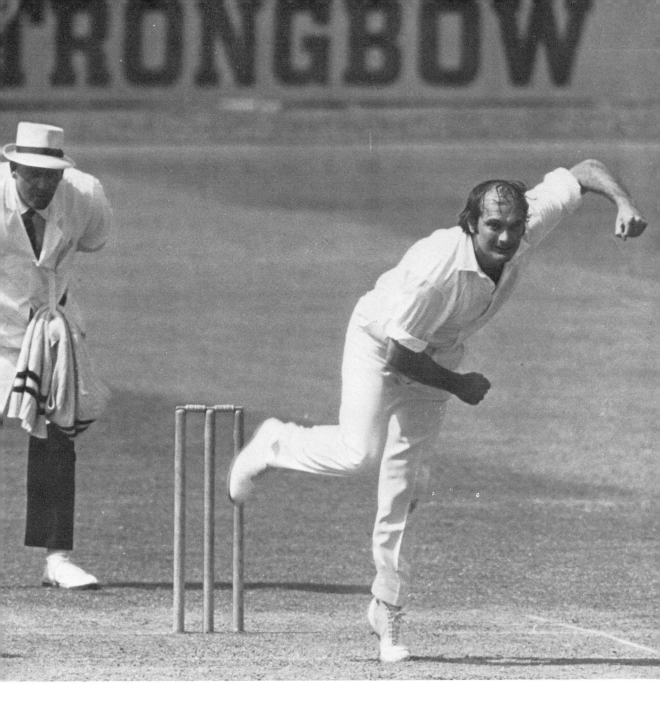

Derek John Somerset Taylor, of Somerset, and Michael Norman Somerset Taylor, of Hampshire, are twins. They were born at Amersham in Buckinghamshire. Derek joined Surrey as a wicketkeeper, but in 1970 moved, with true baptismal sympathy, to Somerset where, under the influence of Brian Close, he became also a good enough batsman to open the innings. Mike went to Nottinghamshire who, inexplicably, did not re-engage him after the 1972 season. Hampshire took him at once. A thoughtful medium pace bowler, capable batsman with appreciable hitting power, a safe fieldsman and a thoroughly intelligent all-round cricketer, he has played some important cricket for his third county.

Vivian Richards
loses his bat to
Max Walker,
Australia v. West
Indies, one-day
International,
Adelaide, 1975.

Yardley is bowled
by Garner,
West Indies v.
Australia, second
Test, Bridgetown,
1978.

Greig is bowled by
Greg Chappell,
England v.
Australia, first
Test, Old Trafford,
1978.

Randall, Australia
v. England, fourth
Test, Sydney, 1979.

The fourth – Sydney – Test between Australia and England in 1978-9 was played in cruelly hot weather even for those regions. There and then Derek Randall came to maturity as a Test batsman, with a highly responsible innings which changed the course of the match. England, who took first innings, were put out for 152, and Australia, with 294, had a substantial lead of 142. Boycott was out, and Randall came in before a run was scored in the second English innings. Australia, conscious that their advantage gave them the chance to square the rubber at two Tests all, attacked to their utmost. Randall batted completely out of his normal

character for almost ten hours, to reshape the innings with a score of 150. Apart from Brearley (53) and Gower (34), no one else made more than 22 in a total of 346 which left Australia 205 to win. Hendrick, Miller and Emburey ensured that they were kept well short of the aim; but only Randall had put them in the position to do so. The camera caught him in the course of that match-winning innings, feeling both the heat and the strain.

The heat of Calcutta during the second Test of 1976-7 was also fierce – even the normally serene Bishen Bedi found the need to cool off from the drinks jug.

Greg Chappell
(centre) batting
during the
Prudential Trophy,
England v.
Australia, The
Oval, 1977.

England had already won the Prudential Trophy rubber of 1977 by taking the
matches at Old Trafford and Edgbaston, before the third at The Oval. Greg Chappell
sent England in to bat and, after an opening stand of 161 by Amiss and Brearley,
Thomson and Pascoe put them out for 242. Australia were 83 for one when rain
stopped play for an hour. When it cleared the captains agreed, since the next day
was Jubilee Day, to play to a finish that evening if possible. In the event it was not
really possible, but they did it. The end – a win for Australia by two wickets,

largely through a masterly 125 not out by Greg Chappell – was achieved in teeming rain with deep puddles on the pitch, and, grotesquely, a blinding sun shining low over the Vauxhall stand. No spectators could stay out in the downpour; and no international match – and few others – can ever have been played in such impossible conditions. If the rubber had been at issue the sides would hardly have gone on: the players and umpires came in with rain streaming through their clothes. No section of the community more completely earned a Jubilee Day holiday.

Mustaq
Mohammad
airborne,
D. H. Robins XI v.
India, Eastbourne,
1974.

OVERLEAF AND
FOLLOWING: Queen's
Park, Savannah.

West Indian cricket is remarkable not only for the amount of cricket played but also for its number of different types of the game. The engaging character in the photograph is on his way out to bat in what is generally known as a beer match, on Trinidad Savannah, which covers a multitude of games.

A beer match is called a beer match because traditionally the players punctuate the action with beer; though some of them take coke, fizzy lemon or even a sly rum.

OVERLEAF: On Accra
Beach, Barbados,
play continues as
long as – or even
longer than – the
light.

Barbados.

Barbados breeds natural cricketers. This photograph was taken at a school where three 'serious' matches were strongly in progress when the teacher opened the door for morning classes.

It is historically true that cricket began in England; that it probably reached its consistently highest level of performance in Australia. In West Indies, however, cricket was the idiom of liberation. It was the vehicle by which people who had risen from slavery expressed their liberty. Nowhere is the game played more spontaneously; more widely; more capably; nor by a greater proportion of the population. Nowhere, ever, in the history of the cricket world has there been such a production of cricket players. The population of Barbados is 311,000, the same as Berkshire. In recent years it has produced – from scratch, the plantations, the byways, the beaches, with no help or advantages – Frank Worrell, Clyde Walcott, Everton Weekes, Seymour Nurse, Garfield Sobers, Roy Marshall, Wesley Hall, Gordon, Geoffrey and Alvin Greenidge, Wayne Daniel, David Murray, Joel Garner, Vanburn Holder, Conrad Hunte, Collis King, John Shepherd, Cammie Smith and Keith Boyce. Few places have known such a fruitful liberation.

English village cricket can be the most orderly kind of combat. A recent match between Hambledon and Steep was played on what has been the original ground of the Hambledon club since the seventeen-forties. Called Broadhalfpenny Down, it slopes away on all sides from the centre, which gave the fieldsmen some long runs in the days when all hits were run out. Now there are clearly marked boundaries.

Broadhalfpenny Down.

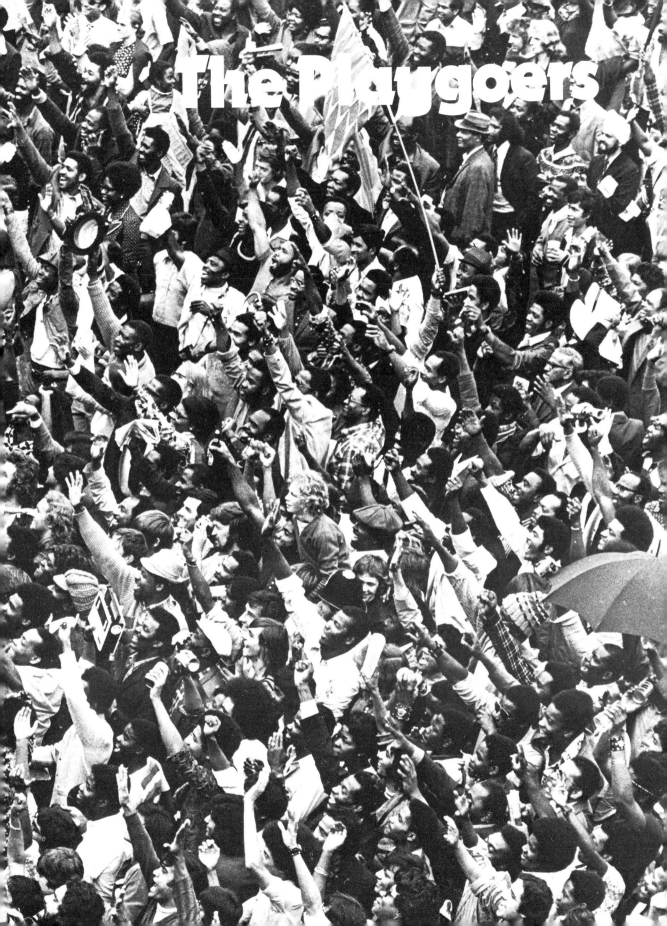

The Playgoers

Beverley Lyon, the controversial and convivial sometime captain of Gloucestershire, had one of the most original brains cricket has known. He thought much about the generalities as well as the strategies and details of the game. 'Cricket,' he once remarked, 'was intended to be played between twenty-two sportsmen for their own pleasure; it was never meant to be the vehicle for international competition, huge crowds and headline news – otherwise it wouldn't have been given a code of laws with such gaps as you could drive through with a coach and horses.' The fact is, though, that it was one of the first spectator games; and has not merely remained so but, through television, has extended its spectatorship to numbers undreamt of between the two wars when the biggest actual 'gates' were gathered.

Societies have been formed of those who watch and follow the game so that its strata extend to arithmetic, reference, biography, bibliography, painting, engraving and writing.

Sometimes, under the influence of play, a crowd can become as one voice. This is especially so when the fielding team is taking wickets rapidly and, as each falls, the killer cry goes up in fierce unison. Apart from a few rare, distant occasions, though, it is only in recent years that, by running on to the field, interfering with players, and even rioting, they have had a seriously adverse effect on play.

Spectators are, of course, necessary in the financial sense. Major cricket could not survive without gate money or, equally important, the fees for television, radio and film rights. The professional spectators, who write about it, have given cricket a literature unequalled by any other sport except bullfighting, and an international news coverage; while the broadcasters have gradually extended their field from sound out into vision which now can be transmitted live across the world.

The first major cricket crowds gathered as long ago as the middle of the eighteenth century. It was to be expected that they were found in London, and in the closely grouped Kentish towns where the game first flourished. They were a phenomenon not always approved. As early as 1743 *The Gentleman's Magazine* reprinted a letter from *The British Champion*:

Of Publick Cricket Matches – The Diversion of Cricket may be proper in Holiday-Time, and in the Country; but upon Days when Men ought to be busy, and in the Neighbourhood of a great City it is not only improper but mischievous in a high Degree. It draws Numbers of People from their Employments, to the Ruin of their Families. It brings together Crowds of Apprentices and Servants, whose Time is not their own. It propagates a Spirit of Idleness at a Juncture, when the utmost Industry, our Debts, Taxes and Decay of Trade, will scarce allow us to get Bread. It is a most notorious Breach of the Laws, as it gives the most open Encouragement to Gaming; the Advertisements most impudently reciting that great Sums are laid; so that some People are so little ashamed of breaking the Laws they had a Hand in making, that they give publick Notice of it.

Although the writer thought cricket proper 'in the Country', it is nevertheless surprising to find large crowds at eighteenth-century matches played on the lonely, bare hills above the Meon valley in Hampshire. Yet Nyren could recall in *The Cricketers of My Time* Hambledon matches on Broadhalfpenny Down: 'Oh! it was a heart-stirring sight to witness the multitude forming a complete and dense circle round that noble green. Half the county would be present, and all their hearts with us.' Or, again: 'There would this company, consisting most likely of

PREVIOUS PAGE:
The crowd at
Lord's, England v.
West Indies, 1973.

some thousands, remain patiently and anxiously watching every turn of fate in the game, as if the event had been the meeting of two armies to decide their liberty.'

Soon, though, the wealthy gentry who had sustained the Hambledon Club found the setting of the cricket too physically and socially bleak. They took their patronage away to London and, henceforth, important cricket matches in England became urban occasions.

In the eighteenth century, Lord's, Prince's and White Conduit and the Honourable Artillery Ground in Finsbury became major London centres and the game, already established in Kent and Sussex, took healthy root in Nottingham and Sheffield. In the eighteen-forties, William Clarke, the one-eyed Nottingham bricklayer who married the widow of the landlord of the Trent Bridge Inn, created 'The All-England Eleven'. This was a travelling team which toured England, Wales, Ireland and Scotland, playing against local eighteens and twenty-twos on dangerous provincial pitches which their players had sometimes to scythe before they were fit for use. They were the – well paid – missionaries of the straight bat and the length ball; they took cricket to small towns which have never seen a team of first class players before or since. They played some seven months of the year for a guarantee, plus a percentage of the invariably appreciable gates. They it was who created a spectator hunger for cricket outside the few major cities which resulted in the creation of the County Championship: W. G. Grace, promptly upon his cue, confirmed and established it. County loyalties were, and still are, strong in English cricket, far transcending the boundaries contrived for the purpose of Local Government Acts. The large towns thrown up by the Industrial Revolution offered the newly-formed county clubs a captive audience of workers during their wakes weeks and, after the passing of the Factory Act in 1850, on their Saturday half holidays.

From the eighteen-seventies Australian cricket, too, became a spectator sport for matches between the 'colonies', but, even more compellingly, for visits of touring teams from England. Soon the Test matches with the opponents they still call 'the Englishmen' or, 'the bloody Poms' became one of the major and senior sporting competitions of the world.

Gradually, spectators increased for matches in South Africa, where the game was prosperously endowed, and West Indies, where it was not. Nowadays the biggest crowds in the world are of another generation of captive audiences, in the Indian sub-continent where Indian and Pakistani matches, particularly against other countries, are the chief sporting occasions of the year.

England during the nineteen-sixties and seventies discovered a 'new' audience drawn by one-day cricket from a section of the community which did not go to county cricket – which subsists on the revenue generated by Test matches – nor to the Tests either. In Australia, Kerry Packer's World Series proved a popular attraction when it recruited most of the best players in the world and deployed them in a series of international matches, with particular success in floodlit evening over-limit play before the television cameras.

Stoppages in play, riots in West Indies, Pakistan and India, have indicated the potential menace to safety in the uninhibited – and often drunken – behaviour of crowds. For a time it seemed that cricket might not suffer so severely as other sports had done; but it has always been too near to the people not to mirror their attitudes. There is no sadder picture in this book than that of young West Indians watching cricket from behind wire netting.

England v. Australia, second Test, Lord's, 1975.

The Long
Room, Lord's.

Lord's, even during a Test match, is an altogether different atmosphere – though so, it must be said, is the Sydney pavilion. Lillee, opening the Australian bowling to Amiss in the second Test of 1975, is watched by a pavilion full of spectators who, whatever the heat, are obliged by club regulations to wear shirts and ties, though there is a tendency, on the top gallery, to remove coats.

Jackets, though, are *de rigeur* in the Long Room, haunt of quiet and privilege, which retains more than a hint of the nineteenth century.

Most engaging of spectators; Neville Cardus, first credited as 'Cricketer' of the *Manchester Guardian* in 1921, wrote on cricket for that paper and for the *Sunday Times* over some fifty years. Proudly a Mancunian, he was the author of some

twenty books about cricket, music and of autobiography. His gift was a capacity to invest cricket and cricketers with a heroic stature: he interpreted the feelings of the literate cricket enthusiast and, in doing so, changed the entire shape of writing about the game.

Ray Robinson, essentially a highly professional journalist on Sydney and Melbourne newspapers, specialised in cricket reporting, covering the Australian scene for *The Cricketer*, *The Times* and *The Observer* and reporting cricket tours for a series of Australian papers. His half-dozen cricket books are among the best written on cricket to come out of Australia – informed, polished, fresh and readable.

Neville Cardus and (below) Ray Robinson.

'Mr. Griffiths',
1973-style Geoff
Boycott supporter.

A Pakistani in
prayer, Lord's,
1974.

Waiting for
Boycott in the rain,
Southampton,
1978.

A bomb scare,
Lord's, 1973.

During the third West Indian Test of 1973, a bomb warning was telephoned to Lord's. Most of the accommodation was cleared. The police who came to search had the power to request – but not to compel – spectators to leave the stands. One in the Tavern stand did not wish to do so – and remained where he was until play was resumed an hour and a half afterwards.

It was Sir Pelham Warner, in many ways an incarnation of Lord's, who wrote 'The sun never sets on cricket'. Eventually its spread has brought teams to his ground from all quarters of the world. In the second England–Pakistan Test of 1974 a Muslim supporter brought out his mat, took off his shoes and knelt to say his prayers on the Nursery ground. It was the match when the covers leaked so that Pakistan, who had left a true wicket, were asked to bat on an impossible one where Underwood was virtually unplayable. Their batsmen – especially Mushtaq – resisted bravely and, happily after such ill luck, more rain, which prevented any play on the last day, gave them the draw which was the least they deserved.

Yorkshiremen in the rain: this elderly man and his grandsons on holiday in southern England travelled to see the Hampshire–Yorkshire match of 1978 at Southampton, only to be caught in the rain.

In 1973, the West Indian 'Mr Griffiths' adopted Geoffrey Boycott and became his 'fan'. Referring to him as 'Sir Geoffrey' he used frequently to proffer amusing and stentorian advice which Boycott acknowledged amiably.

Boycott out –
c. Kanhai b. Holder,
England v. West
Indies, third Test,
Lord's, 1973.

In the third – Lord's – Test of 1973, some young West Indian supporters boisterously celebrated the dismissal of Boycott – caught by Kanhai off Holder for four – after West Indies had declared at 652 for eight. (They went on to win by an innings and 226 runs – their widest margin against England.) Lord's generally has employed stewards, police, the threat of ejection and the atmosphere of 'Head-quarters' to keep crowds in order.

The Headingley crowd at the fourth Australian Test of 1977 celebrated both England winning The Ashes, and Geoffrey Boycott's hundredth hundred – though not necessarily in that order of precedence.

When Geoffrey Boycott reached his hundredth century – the first man to do so in a Test match – against Australia at Headingley in 1977, a bunch of hooligans ran on to the pitch, slapping him violently on the back, stealing his cap and replacing it with a paper hat. A loudspeaker appeal elicited the return of the cap, but such treatment must be likely to break a batsman's concentration; and it is much to Boycott's credit that he batted on so soundly. For many years cricketers returning to the old pavilion at Headingley had to do so through a long corridor, stretching far out on to the ground, formed by youngsters who presumed to pat them on the back until, often, they came in with their shirts black from their own sweat and the youngsters' grime.

RIGHT: Headingley, 1977.

England v.
Australia, fourth
Test, The Oval,
1975.

England v.
Australia, second
Test, Lord's, 1975.

Pakistan v. India,
second Test,
Lahore, 1977-8.

The ordinances at The Oval are specific.

It is doubtful, though, if any noticeboard would have deterred the streaker who ran on to the Lord's pitch during the second England–Australia Test of 1975. He was arrested, partly covered, taken away, and charged. Next morning he was fined at the local magistrate's court.

Everything happens to Greig. At the luncheon interval in the one-day International at Melbourne in 1974, two girls in bikinis ran on to the pitch and, as reported, 'presented him with a bunch of flowers'.

The scoreboard at Lahore – second Pakistan–India Test of 1977-8 – despite the suggestion of his followers Zaheer scored only 235 not out.

Australia v. England, one-day International, Melbourne, 1974.

123

Outside and inside
the ground,
Canterbury, 1974.

'The Canterbury breakfast' has become something of a Kentish occasion since the county's series of successes – eight championships, two losing finals and two Fenner Trophies – in one-day cricket. Some spectators began to queue outside the St. Lawrence Ground at Canterbury as early as half-past ten the night before their Gillette Cup semi-final with Somerset in 1974; and quite a substantial lane of cars had formed by 6.45 a.m. The first of the waiting crowd are admitted at half-past seven, when there is a seemly semi-rush to reserve their special places.

After the long wait, eight o'clock is time for breakfast. Eggs and bacon and coffee are cooked behind one of the cars in one of the coveted, front-row positions from which it is possible to watch the play. Of old, members, allowed to ride their horses into the ground, often reined them in to watch from the same north-western bank where the motors now stand.

St. Lawrence, aptly called 'the Goodwood of cricket', is the only first class ground in England with a tree standing inside the playing area; a ball that hits it counts four and is dead; a batsman cannot be caught or run out off it. It stands in the corner of the ground where the club marquees – up to a dozen or more – are pitched. They afford refreshment, a comfortable seat and, at need, shelter.

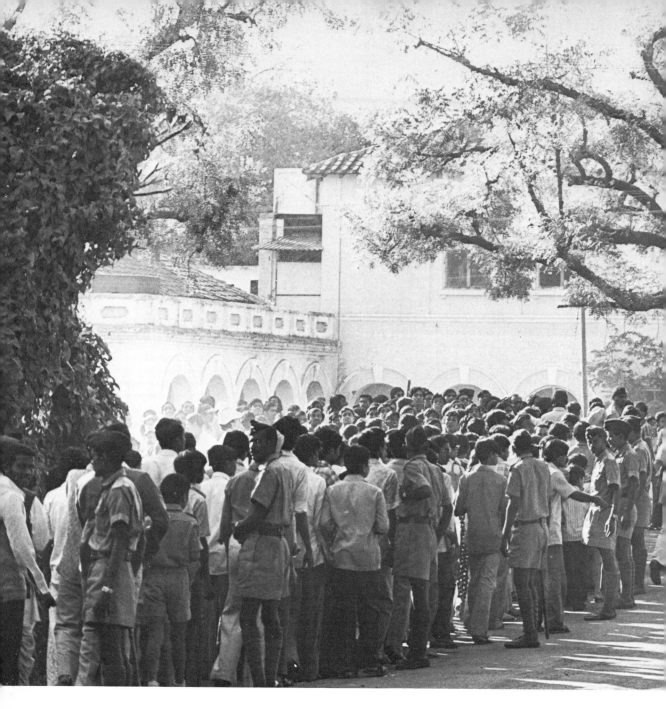

The vast population of India and the low proportion of car ownership ensures crowds for matches which would attract few in England or Australia. On their tour of 1977, M.C.C. played Combined Universities of India at Nagpur. A touring team's comparable fixture in England would barely pay its own expenses. At Nagpur there was not only a large crowd – gathering by bus, on cycles or on foot – to watch the match; but they even queued afterwards in the hope of catching sight of the players as they drove away in their bus.

Checking the tickets at Nagpur is a responsible task, to be carried out by a uniformed official.

Outside and inside, Nagpur, 1977.

India v. England
second Test,
Calcutta, 1977.

The second Test of 1976-7 between India and England was played at Eden Gardens, Calcutta. The official figure for a 'full house' there is 70,000; but unofficial estimates put it at 100,000, and suggest that the Melbourne 'record' is frequently exceeded. On some occasions there have clearly been more than a hundred photographers present, of whom less than 20 were *bona fide* professionals. A vast number of passes are issued and many of them are used for more than one person.

Making the simple best of two worlds, the East of ancient days combines with European machinery of fifty years ago in the mowing of the outfield at Karachi before the third Pakistan–England Test of 1977-8.

India *v.* England, second Test of 1976-7, at Calcutta; an umpire joins in the supervision of the ground staff rolling the wicket.

Pakistan v.
England, third
Test, Karachi,
1978.

India v. England,
second Test,
Calcutta, 1976-7.

Crowd control netting which runs all round the ground, except in front of the pavilion, prevents any incursions on to the pitch. West Indies v. Australia, Kensington Oval, Barbados, 1973.

Between India and
Pakistan, 1978.

In 1978-9, Test matches between Pakistan and India were resumed after a gap of
seventeen years, which included a war between the two countries. It is normally
difficult – and involves a long wait – for Indian citizens to obtain visas to enter
Pakistan. For the duration of the Tests, however, they were promptly available on
the basis of a one-day clearance on production of a day-ticket; eight days for a
match-ticket. The four Indian Sikhs in the photograph had just crossed the border
near their homes at Amritsar without difficulty on their way to the Lahore Test.

A crowd-study providing at Eastern parallel with Frith's Derby Day. The crowds
making their way home in the evening after play in the second India–England
Calcutta crowds . . . Test of 1977 at Calcutta.

There is a modern stand at Madras but, for the third Test with England in 1976–7, a temporary gallery was built out of readily available materials.

The atmosphere of West Indian cricket is electric, excitable, but usually tinged with humour. A study of the crowd at Bridgetown, Barbados in 1973.

Test matches are among the rare occasions on which Moslem women may now go out unchaperoned in public in Pakistan. In the second Pakistan–India Test of 1977–8, in Lahore, the ladies were sufficiently informed to applaud the dismissal of the leading Indian batsman, Sunil Gavaskar.

A misty impression of nostalgia. The former pavilion at Fenner's, Cambridge; pleasing and full of memories. Now demolished, it has been replaced, at the other end of the ground, by an unmemorable building which serves as a pavilion.

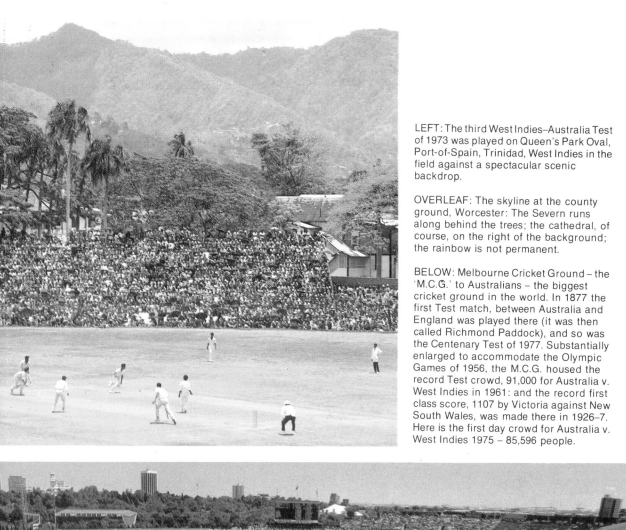

LEFT: The third West Indies–Australia Test of 1973 was played on Queen's Park Oval, Port-of-Spain, Trinidad, West Indies in the field against a spectacular scenic backdrop.

OVERLEAF: The skyline at the county ground, Worcester: The Severn runs along behind the trees; the cathedral, of course, on the right of the background; the rainbow is not permanent.

BELOW: Melbourne Cricket Ground – the 'M.C.G.' to Australians – the biggest cricket ground in the world. In 1877 the first Test match, between Australia and England was played there (it was then called Richmond Paddock), and so was the Centenary Test of 1977. Substantially enlarged to accommodate the Olympic Games of 1956, the M.C.G. housed the record Test crowd, 91,000 for Australia v. West Indies in 1961: and the record first class score, 1107 by Victoria against New South Wales, was made there in 1926–7. Here is the first day crowd for Australia v. West Indies 1975 – 85,596 people.

Australia v. West
Indies, Sydney
Cricket Ground,
1976.

The gathering of
cans.

Kerry Packer's
World Series
Cricket – Sydney
Cricket Ground,
January 1979.

The crowd inside Sydney Cricket Ground for the fourth Test with West Indies in
January 1976 is identifiably Australian by the 'Eskies' – cases for the cooled
transport of canned beer – carried by most of the spectators. The 'Eskies' can
be, and often are, refilled from the bars inside the ground.

'The Hill' at Sydney has a reputation for its barrackers. Courteous visiting
reporters used to refer to their 'wit', but there is no longer any pretence of
maintaining that inaccurate compliment. As can be imagined by the distribution
of 'Eskies', and the heat, there is an extremely high incidence of drunkenness,
which militates against anything so sharp as wit, but finds its outlets in abuse.

Towards the end of the day The Hill is a brewer's delight; the atmosphere
beerily warm and noisy.

The gathering of the cans is a considerable daily operation, providing casual
employment. The final harvest is a sobering thought; certainly a wry comment on
a civilisation.

The Players

The Players on Tour

The players are everyone who ever picked up bat or ball in the elementary game of 'casting a ball at three straight sticks and defending the same with a fourth'. Cricket is truly a people's game. It is not divisive as, in their different fashions, association, rugby and rugby league football are. Cricket is played by men, by women, and, perhaps most purely of all, by children. It is played by all classes; among them kings and princes of England (including one who probably left the earliest known record of the game as 'creag'), by slaves, by children in back streets, with rolled rag for a ball, a stick for a bat and a wicket chalked on a wall.

At the top of the performing scale, some few hundred men are, by news values, 'the players'. Once there was a division between amateur and professional expressed in the match played in England for over a century and called Gentlemen *versus* Players; of which it was said 'of course all the players are gentlemen, but...'

Cricket is a most precarious profession; it is called a team game but, in fact, no one is so lonely as a batsman facing a bowler supported by ten fieldsmen and observed by two umpires to ensure that his error does not go unpunished. There is, too, the loneliness of the deep fieldsman under a high catch, which is swirling in the wind. Consider, too, the bowler who must send down the last ball, with the result of the match turning on it, and a well set batsman at the other end.

These stresses apply at all levels; but at the top a career depends on such hazards. Yet men have accepted this as a profession – in truth, a life – even though, until quite lately, the financial returns were good only for perhaps a dozen of the great; and there simply was no security for anyone. It exerts a strange compulsion over its devotees; and, great performers or rabbits, they are all the same in the mind and the heart.

The professional cricketer's life is unique in many ways. In none, though, does it differ more from the styles of other sportsmen than in the overseas tour. It is a major point to any cricketer's credit that he is 'a good tourist'. When teams went by sea between England, India, Australia, New Zealand and South Africa, they might leave in September and not return until the following April, or vice versa. Even now an English tour in Australia lasts four months. Some authorities set their faces against wives accompanying husbands, so do some players; others have said in the witness box that absence from their wives makes them dislike tours. Even when wives do make a tour they may only sometimes stay with their husbands; but never join in team activities. Normal touring life is a strange, communal existence. It is always said – and there is considerable evidence for it – that a touring team develops a unity and a sense of purpose that a home side rarely has. It is true, though, that rivalry, competition for Test places, relative form and varying success can build up bitterness within a party.

Some find the travelling, the weather, or unaccustomed food problems; and for many senior players it is a case of *déja vu*. Generally for those making their first trips – and always for some – it is an absorbing experience. Especially in India and Pakistan the players are fêted like royalty and everywhere they encounter generous hospitality.

The short walk from the Eden Gardens ground to the Grand Hotel, Calcutta, pushing through the massed, inquisitive, but not hostile crowds, can be an arduous physical strain.

Mike Brearley,
Old Trafford, 1977.

The picture taken over the shoulder of Sarfraz Narwaz in the mini-bus taking him from the ground after play in the second 1978 Test at Lahore shows the admiring, curious crowds who ask no more than to look at the players.

Press conferences have become an increasingly important and demanding ingredient of the touring captain's life. Not everyone does it well, but Mike Brearley has usually combined a courteous good humour with the right degrees of frankness and tact, consideration and elucidation, brevity and adequacy. He was understandably happy when the press of both countries met him after England had beaten Australia at Old Trafford in 1977.

Touring time-tables are now based on air journeys. In flight between Perth and Adelaide in the 1978-9 tour, Doug Insole's mind was obviously far indeed from the cards which engaged Emburey, Gower, Miller, Botham and Randall.

Talking tactics; Boycott and Brearley in The Oval dressing room 1977 at the end of the Australian series. Bats, some signed, some awaiting signature, cover the tables.

146

A player's view, here Sarfraz Nawaz's, Pakistan v. India, second Test, Lahore, 1978.

The 1978-9 tour, in flight between Perth and Adelaide.

Boycott and Brearley in the Oval dressing room, 1977.

Melbourne,
Christmas Day,
1974.

Twelfth man John
Lever, Lord's,
1978.

Modern hotel life furnishes the touring cricketers with a greatly relished diversion in the swimming pool; Jeff Thomson at the Hilton Hotel, Port of Spain, Trinidad.

Several players brought out their wives and families during the English tour of Australia in 1974-5. On Christmas Day 1974, the day before the Melbourne Test began, Underwood, Fletcher, Greig and Amiss helped with the children's party.

Christmas at the Melbourne Hilton 1978. Every member of the English team was allotted a letter of the alphabet as initial to the costume he might choose to wear. Ian Botham drew G – and plumped for gorilla.

Twelfth man's chores include passing round bats and books to be autographed. At least, though, he has ample time to sign for himself; John Lever, indeed, had far too much time on his hands as constant twelfth man during 1978.

FAR LEFT : Jeff
Thomson, Trinidad,
1978.

TOP RIGHT :
Christmas Day,
Melbourne, 1978.

149

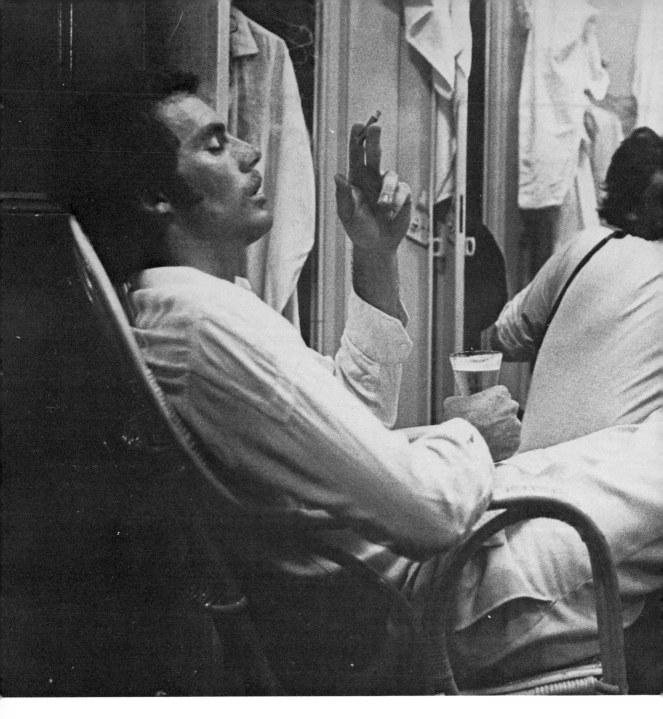

The Players at Play

The pictures chosen for the following section are of The Players – not an attempt to catalogue the all-time greats, nor even the best players of the last twenty years or so, but a selection of cricketers whom I happen to have photographed. Some are almost impossible to take well and in one or two cases I confess to having given up trying – their photographs do not appear here.

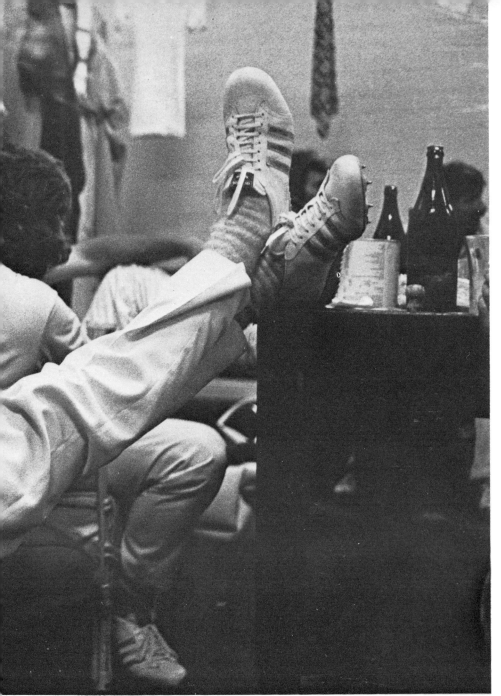

Greg Chappell
relaxes after
Australia won the
Ashes, Sydney,
1975.

It is an opportunity to include modern portraits of players who were at their
peak long before I was born, with names that read straight from the pages of
cricket history; Woolley, Fender, Sutcliffe, Grimmett, Bradman and Larwood
being perhaps the most evocative. In the main it is a collection of the more
photogenic cricketers of the sixties and seventies.

P.E.

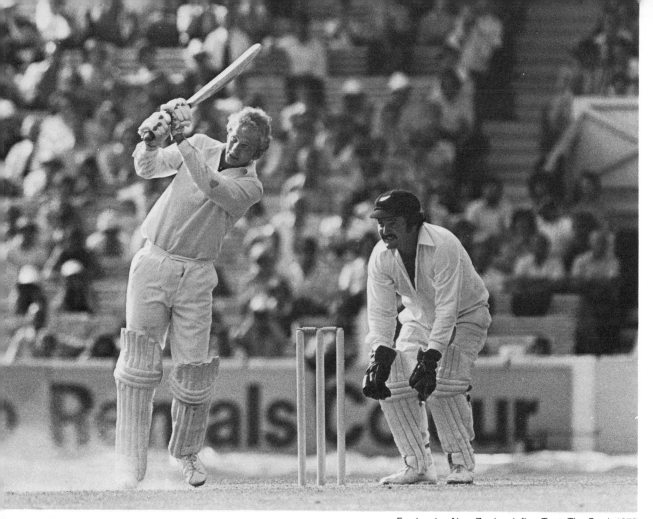

England v. New Zealand, first Test, The Oval, 1978.

David Gower

From time to time a cricketer springs up in England who warms the hearts of those who think that neither the game nor its players are what they used to be. Happily enough, when the English cricket establishment and its supporters were most anxious about the Packer defections, two such young men appeared. One was David Gower; the other, Ian Botham.

David Gower must be regarded as one of the remarkable post-war harvest of talent of Kent. A left-hander, he was born at Tunbridge Wells, went to school at King's Canterbury and was taken to Loughborough when his family settled there.

Of course Leicestershire soon learnt about him; and, when Kent raised no objections, they registered him. His talent was so obvious that everyone who saw him realised that his entry to the top class was no more than a matter of time – and probably of little time, at that. He had his first county game at nineteen. Under Illingworth he

was steered to the certain end of international cricket – at twenty-one. As soon as he came on the Test scene he hooked his first ball – from Liaqat Ali – for four.

David Gower is slim, wiry, apparently not tense; and he has superb wrists. There is about him an air of growing up with an innate wisdom about batting – not a know-all, but a born understander. He is quiet, modest but clear-minded, and he has a quick sense of humour. He plays his own game. Perhaps the years will lead him to greater caution; for the moment he looks a natural batsman who hits the ball that seems hittable, though he sometimes plays, over-confidently, across the line. He hooks with the same almost languid certainty as he drives through the covers. He gave himself such a fine start that, even at twenty-one, he was accepted by cricketing England as a fixed star for a couple of decades to come. That, surely, is a sound judgment.

Ian Botham

The second of England's new cricketing heroes, Ian Botham, was, like Maurice Tremlett before him, born in Cheshire, but settled as a cricketer in Somerset. Like Tremlett, too, he attracted attention early by his form as a pace bowler, attacking batsman and close fielder. Tremlett, though, had some unsympathetic handling in his early days and did not fulfil his potential as a bowler, though he became a capable batsman and an outstanding captain.

Ian Botham is a young giant; filled with a fine impatience, powerful but mobile; a thinking athlete with an impelling urge to succeed. He has more than made good the loss of Greig to the English team. As a batsman he is upstanding, powerful, aggressive. A flighty slow bowler may tempt him into impatience; but anyone of any pace who bowls anything loose to him may expect it to be hit ferociously. He learnt much in that great coaching school at Lord's; and the best aspect of his bowling is his late outswing at medium to fast-medium; but it is by no means all

of it. His strong, full, body action enables him to generate such pace that it was held at Taunton, during the 1978 Whit match with Gloucestershire, that probably only Willis of current English bowlers was faster than Botham when he cared to concentrate on speed. He can bowl a sharp bouncer; and a well disguised slower ball which turns from the off. The ball sinks comfortably and safely into his large hands at slip, short leg or wherever else he finds himself. He is an explosive cricketer; a success man. He first appeared for Somerset in 1974 when he was eighteen, was capped by the county in 1976, by England in 1977; and scored his first Test century in 1978. When he has 'come off' in Tests it has invariably been with five wickets in an innings, or a century. Already, by the end of the Australian series of 1978-9, he was eating up the statistical race track for young batsmen and bowlers. He is a splendid, lusty competitor with plenty of strength to keep him going for many years in the upper brackets of cricketing achievement.

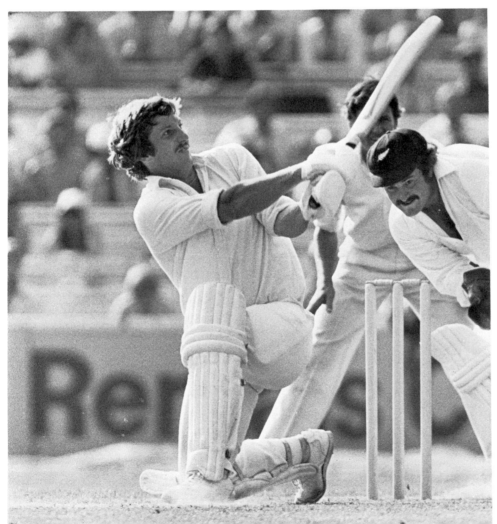

England v. New Zealand, first Test, The Oval, 1978.

153

Derek Randall

On the cricket field Derek Randall is a Pinocchio figure, searching for truth, all twitches, restlessness, excitements, anxieties and clowning. In fact, he is a happy extrovert, who clowns spontaneously. He is also as effective as he is entertaining in the field; a batsman of gifts sufficient to compensate for his technical flaws, and an authority which has grown with his sense of responsibility. There was a time when he did not seem to take cricket seriously; and certainly some shrewd judges did not take him seriously, while others thought of him as a one-day, over-limit player.

He went on the India tour of 1976-7 as a reserve batsman; came in for the second Test because others fell out, and, for the same reason, played through the rubber for the meagre average of 12.30 from seven innings. So he was fortunate

that his form – or others' lack of it – took him into the side for the Centenary Test at Melbourne. There he reached the peak of his career. Against an Australian attack short only of Thomson, and, when England needed 463 to win, he played an innings at once skilful, brave, attractive, jaunty and humorous, to make 174, and bring them within sight of victory. Once, when Lillee bowled a steep bouncer at him, he smashed it tennis-fashion to midwicket for four; he ducked another, straightened up, raised his cap and bowed to the bowler; felled by a short ball from Lillee, he turned a full somersault. The crowd, already delighted by his fielding, accepted him with delight as their man; and he played to them without ever relaxing in concentration upon his batting.

So he came back to England cast in a heroic role

Randall hooks for 4 off Hogg to bring up his century, Australia v. England, fourth Test, Sydney, 1979.

The Randall cartwheel at the moment when England retained The Ashes at Headingley in 1977 is well known. Here is one performed out of sheer high spirits during a dull passage of play at Nagpur in 1977. The crowd there enjoyed him, too.

and, against Australia, he played usefully at Lord's and brightly at Old Trafford but then fell away in the rest of the series. It seemed that he simply could not stand still as the bowler came in, but shuffled across his stumps precisely when he should have been stationary.

The shuffle continued through an indifferent tour of Pakistan and New Zealand in 1977-8, with an average of 19 for nine Tests. The selectors were appalled: and they left him out of the home series of 1978 against Pakistan and New Zealand, with the message that, before he was considered again for selection, he had to show solid consistency in the county game. He did, most certainly, bat responsibly and diligently for Nottinghamshire to average 44, although with only one century; and was given the last batting place in the touring side only narrowly from

Tavaré. Once in Australia, and after Radley had been bounced out of consideration, Randall had another chance, and took it like a mature cricketer with a century against New South Wales, 75 and 74 not out (the two highest English innings) in the first Test, when he was named Man of the Match; and the highly responsible 150 which first turned, and then won, the fourth. He still shuffles across his stumps but, thanks to his good eye, he seems to have learnt to compensate for it, and it does give him greater opportunity to employ his profitable leg-side strokes; but it calls for considerable adjustment, and is so fundamentally technically incorrect that it could yet cause him much trouble. Meanwhile Derek Randall continues – exuberant, acrobatic, enthusiastic, and as popular as any cricketer in the world.

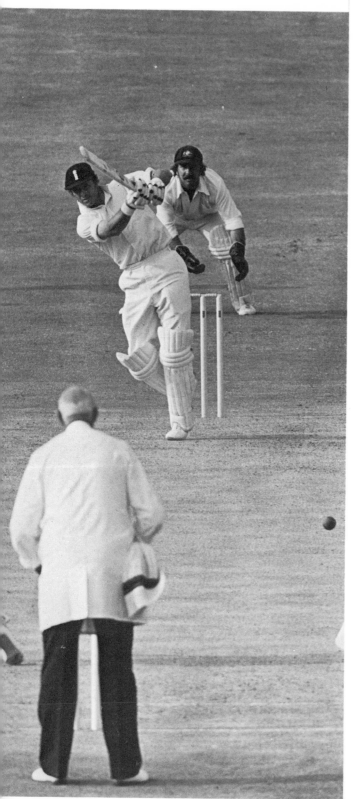

Geoffrey Boycott

Geoffrey Boycott has always been a solitary; a perfectionist batsman, determined to succeed, and succeeding. He tasted county cricket and tested himself there before he committed himself to it as a career. Once he had taken that decision, no training, no practice, no preparation was too minute or detailed for his unremitting attention. His progress was rapid; a first appearance for Yorkshire in 1962 (at 21), a county cap in 1963, first appearance for England, 1964, and, thereafter, a regular Test place, except once when he was dropped from one match for slow scoring (246 not out in 573 minutes) or declared himself unavailable. He played first in spectacles and then, with painstaking preparation, in contact lenses.

At times, notably when he scored two centuries in the Test Trial at Worcester in 1974, he seemed almost to eliminate risk from batting.

Nettled by the West Indian fast bowlers of 1973 into hooking injudiciously, he dealt with them capably in their own country in the following winter. Then, after the Indian slow-medium left-arm bowler, Solkar, had taken his wicket four times in 1974, he declared himself unavailable for England. It was the fury of the perfectionist at discovery of a flaw. He did not return until 1977, when he replaced Amiss for the third Australian Test, at Trent Bridge, and scored 107. He went on to the historic achievement of completing his hundred centuries in a Test against Australia in front of the Yorkshire crowd at Headingley; and in his three Tests of that season he averaged 147.33.

He was appointed captain of Yorkshire in 1971, and there was some controversy within the county when he was not reappointed for 1979. The matter was apparently resolved when, with more grace than any other party to the matter, he accepted a two-year contract to play under Jackie Hampshire. In fact, because of their deep concentration on their batting, the great batsmen have rarely been outstanding as captains; and Boycott, above all, is one who should be left free to devote himself completely to his innings.

Geoffrey Boycott has taken the rough knocks to be expected by one who stays so determinedly on the line, including fractures of an arm and several fingers. He has, too, suffered from the interest of the media; and he has not always understood the rest of the world. Whatever else may be said of him, he will be remembered as an utterly dedicated cricketer. He has always said that he is

Boycott drives for his 100th century, England v. Australia, fourth Test, Headingley, 1977.

prepared to allow his figures to speak for him, and they show that he has scored more runs in first class cricket than any other current player, and more in Tests than anyone else now active except Rohan Kanhai; and no doubt he expects to pass him soon. He has the time – and, surely, still the purpose – to go yet further.

Alan Knott

Before Alan Knott joined W.S.C., he had placed himself comfortably statistically clear of all other Test wicketkeepers with 252 dismissals. The division between 233 catches and 19 stumpings is a commentary on the shape of the modern game; the Australian Bertie Oldfield, in the inter-war period, made 78 catches and 52 stumpings.

Knott is a busy and diligent wicketkeeper; invariably fit; so concerned to keep himself loose that he constantly carries out stretching and bending exercises while he is on the field.

A fine wicketkeeper; perpetually alert, far ranging in his hunger for catches, and studiously secure of hand, he suffered so much from the stresses of his position that he seemed to lose his appetite for the game. To join Packer certainly gave him the longest relief from the strain of first class cricket that he had known. The pressure on a wicketkeeper probably is greater than that on other players. Knott suffered it without unloading it on colleagues or acquaintances; but it was long apparent that he did not aspire to a whole career of tension.

He bore, too, a considerable burden as a batsman in a period when the England batting was thin, and much responsibility descended on him. His reaction was characteristically bold and resourceful, but it added to his trauma. He alone challenges Leslie Ames – also of Kent – as the finest of wicketkeeper-batsmen.

Rowe becomes Knott's 220th Test victim – a new record, England v. West Indies, fifth Test, The Oval, 1976.

England v. Australia, fifth Test, Old Trafford, 1977.

Bob Willis

The international cricket power struggle hinges largely on the possession of heavy artillery – the fast bowlers. So Bob Willis has been an asset not only to England's bowling, but to their batsmen.

He catches the eye on the field. Six feet six tall, rangy, wide-shouldered, strong-legged, with a shock of red-brown hair, he looks like the fast bowler he always wanted to be. His action is not ideal and it probably has contributed to some of the many physical troubles he has experienced – knee damage, strained stomach muscles, sore heels, blistered toes, and back trouble – all of which he has tackled by demanding surgery and carrying out fatiguing drills and exercises – often over long periods – to come back again. He is an eager bowler, not quite so fast as some, but unquestionably fast; always attacking and regarding himself as free to use the bouncer when he wishes. Given only a little pace in the pitch, he will worry most batsmen and, from time to time, he makes the ball come back off the pitch quite disconcertingly.

Brought up near Guildford, he joined Surrey in 1969 as a twenty-year-old. A year later, when Alan Ward broke down, he was flown out to Australia where he played a significant part in Illingworth's side that won The Ashes. Apart from his dozen wickets he batted usefully at crucial periods; and held some catches with a speed and mobility surprising in one so long-limbed. When, on his return, he could not find a first-team place with Surrey, he left them and, after some objections and difficulties, joined Warwickshire where he rapidly won a cap, shared in a Championship win and settled contentedly. Bob Willis is not only a keen cricketer; he thinks perceptively about both the game and his fellow players. Hence his appointment as vice-captain of England; hence, too, his extra value to the team.

Canterbury,
County
Championship,
Kent v. Sussex,
1976.

Derek Underwood

In the dressing rooms of the world Derek Underwood is known as 'Deadly'; which may sound funny, but is no joke. It has been said, with full justification, that, for over a decade, captains of England carried him around like an umbrella, in case of rain.

Once he overcame a lack of confidence against left-handers, he was clearly a world-class bowler. The machine-like accuracy of his orthodox left-arm spin and cut at about medium pace make him a sound defensive bowler on good pitches at Test level; a highly effective brake in the county game, and a match-winner in over-limit play. On a rain affected or dusty wicket, though, he has always been a unique killer. Giving the ball no air, and the batsman no time to step up to it,

dropping with remorseless accuracy about middle, middle-and-off according to the response of the wicket, he turns sharply away from the bat, often with vicious lift. Before he was 26 he had taken a thousand wickets (only George Lohmann and Wilfred Rhodes have done that when younger) and his two-hundredth Test wicket at thirty.

A game batsman – and always a volunteer for the night watch – he has played some useful innings for a tail ender; and he is a faithful fielder at mid-on or mid-off. Fresh-faced, frank and keen, he has been the best kind of young cricketer – and a spectacular destroyer; no one else of his kind and quality is to be seen.

Brian Close is hit by a bouncer from Daniel, England v. West Indies, third Test, Old Trafford, 1976.

Brian Close

Of all famous cricketers' careers, Brian Close's is least to be appreciated from its figures. To be sure, he has achieved some remarkable feats; in his first season, with Yorkshire, when he was only eighteen, he performed the double and became the youngest man ever to play in a Test for England.

As a left-hand batsman he could, at need, defend most doggedly, but he preferred to attack, and in full cry he was a glorious stroke-maker in the classic manner, with the strength to strike mighty sixes. He bowled either right-arm, medium-pace outswing, or slow off-breaks, and

in the dressing rooms he was jokingly called 'golden arm' because of his uncanny knack, as a change bowler, of taking good wickets with indifferent deliveries. He fielded brilliantly and fearlessly at slip and shortleg, where he held some amazing catches; and his career figures of 34,824 runs, 1,116 wickets and 808 catches indicate performances of constant value. He was a ruthless and tactically – if not psychologically – shrewd captain in the Yorkshire mould; they won the County Championship four times and, although he did not care for the one-day game, the Gillette Cup twice during his nine years of office. He made decisions quickly – often over-hastily – and, once he made them, he stuck to them through thick and thin. His judgment was, we must say, by no means always sound. When, at nineteen, he went to Australia with F. R. Brown, he scored a century in the first match and then, in his only Test of the tour, twice destroyed himself – and England's chances – with 0 and 1. Many influential figures in the game did not forgive him for having, as they saw it, lost the Old Trafford Test of 1961 – and the rubber with it – by an injudicious attack on Benaud's bowling. While he held the post of England captain, the T.C.C.B. Disciplinary Committee found him guilty of, and censured him for, deliberately wasting time in a match between Yorkshire and Warwickshire at Edgbaston. Close's stated reaction was that, in the same circumstances he would do the same again, and – for that attitude, not the original offence – he was relieved of the England captaincy. When Yorkshire terminated his engagement at the end of the 1970 season, he joined Somerset, was capped at once; and made captain a year later. Over the next six years he did much to mould the character of the side of mounting power which Brian Rose took over in 1978.

Brian Close was possessed of a fine fury; impatient of defeat or frustration, he sought to dominate opponents. He would stand dangerously close at short leg and once, after a batsman had been caught in the gully off a rebound from Close's forehead, he was asked 'But what if it had hit you in the temple?' he answered: 'Then he would have been caught at slip.' He took a monumental beating from the West Indian fast bowlers, Hall and Griffiths in 1963; and, called back to face their even more menacing successors, Roberts, Holding, Daniel, Julien and Holder in 1976, when he was 44 years old, he batted with equal courage, once making top score and three times highest but one, in a routed team.

Derek Shackleton

In the twenty-one years between 1948 and 1969, Derek Shackleton took more wickets – 2,857 (an average of 130 a season) – than any other post-war bowler. He was born in Todmorden which is, by a little distance, in Yorkshire. Hampshire signed him after the war as a promising young batsman who sometimes bowled leg breaks. One day, desperately short of seam bowlers, the county

Derek Shackleton, Hampshire v. South Africans, Southampton, 1965.

sent every member of the staff into the nets to see what they could do in that direction. Derek Shackleton showed some degree of talent and within a year became a major county bowler.

He was a remarkable performer. Twenty years in succession he took a hundred wickets in the season. His approach was lightfooted as a dancing master's; he brought his arm over – wrist sharply cocked – with a swing so smooth it seemed that his shoulder joint must be on well-oiled ball bearings. It all looked so easy that it concealed his pace, which could be lively fast medium. By constant experiment he mastered both swings, cut the ball both ways and had more variations than all but two of his wicketkeepers could regularly fathom.

His length was so immaculate and so regular that a few hitters – Fred Trueman was one – punished him by hitting exactly where they thought he would pitch. 'Shack' always applauded anyone who hit him for six – he knew that retribution was near; his great haul of wickets cost on average only 18.65 apiece. Nothing ruffled him or his hair and no bowler now active is within sight of his number of wickets.

Colin Cowdrey

Only nine batsmen made more runs in first class cricket than Colin Cowdrey's 42,719 at 42.89, with 107 centuries; and all but two of those who lead him took more innings to do it. He played in the record number of 114 Tests for an aggregate of 7,624, exceeded only by Garfield Sobers. Yet there remains a feeling that he might have achieved even more. Few players made batting look so simple. Certainly he could have played more than he did, especially in the three or four seasons towards the end of his 26-year career. It seemed, too, that he was less assertive, even less competitive, than others not so capable.

He was a schoolboy prodigy; at the age of thirteen he went in first wicket down for Tonbridge against Clifton at Lord's, scored 75 and 44 and, by taking the last five Clifton wickets with his leg-breaks, won the match in a close finish. He was less than a fortnight past his twenty-second birthday when he scored 102 – out of a total of 191 – to keep England in the third Melbourne Test of 1954-5, a match which they eventually won. A placid, unhurried, slip fieldsman of such fast reflexes that all catches looked simple to him, he had all the gifts; and he made batting a joy to watch.

He was not always lucky; after establishing himself as England captain by his sympathetic and successful handling of the side in West Indies in 1967-8, he had the misfortune to be injured on his return to England. Illingworth succeeded him with such impressive results that Cowdrey, to his immense and understandable disappointment, never regained the appointment. He accepted some beatings by the fast bowlers with phlegmatic calm; and was one of the few of the target men who never cracked.

Consider this photo. Cowdrey had left home in an English December only six days before he went in to bat in the second Test at Perth. Yet, here he is, steering Lillee – bowling at full pace on the fast Perth wicket – away to third man with the calm, contemplative air of a man playing with children. More perhaps than any other cricketer he conveyed the impression of time to spare in playing his strokes; almost as if he were lecturing on the making of the stroke as he executed it. He was indeed a master.

Basil D'Oliveira

Only another coloured South African can appreciate the magnitude of Basil D'Oliveira's achievement. He feared it was already too late, when his cricketing ability enabled him – by a desperately narrow margin – to escape from the second-rate citizen's life he lived in the Cape. He came to England, played league cricket – successfully after some frightening initial problems on his first encounter with English turf wickets – for Worcestershire, became a British citizen, was capped for England, scored five Test centuries, was twice in an England side that won or retained The Ashes and, in the 1969 Birthday Honours List, was made an O.B.E.

He was not even eligible to play county cricket until his middle thirties, yet he appeared in 44 Tests, always capably and – especially against high pace – bravely; sometimes decisively. A right-hand bat, he is, for a self-taught player, quite orthodox in defence; he has, though, so little back lift as made the power of some of his driving quite phenomenal. As a bowler, he mixes off spin with cutters and floaters at slow medium to medium pace. As he has grown older, he has lost his former mobility in the field, but his hands are always safe. Relaxed, cheerful and courteous, he never flapped; and, although the attempts were made to involve him in some racial and political controversies, he behaved with unfailing dignity. For one who came to the first class game so late, his figures of 18,000 runs, 540 wickets and over 200 catches are impressive. He was in two Championship-winning Worcestershire sides and one which won the John Player League, once in a Gillette, and twice in a Benson & Hedges final. His value in the over-limit game is indicated by his record of six Gillette Man of the Match and two Benson & Hedges gold awards. He has several times vowed his intention to retire from active play and take up coaching, but so far its attraction and Worcestershire's strategic need have drawn him back. In 1976 he went quietly determined to the Benson & Hedges final against Kent at Lord's. Gifford put Kent in to bat and D'Oliveira severely damaged a hamstring in the field. Worcestershire needed 237 to win and D'Oliveira came in, at 90 for four, with a runner and able only to stand firm-footed at the crease. Yet he made 50, Worcestershire's top score, mainly by fours and a six, in 14 overs, before he was bowled driving at Jarvis.

Worcestershire v. Leicestershire, Gillette Cup, Worcester, 1973.

163

John Edrich

For twenty years John Edrich was the hardest man in England to get out. Born at Blofield into the famous Norfolk cricketing family, he played a Minor Counties season for his native county before he joined Surrey in 1955: and went back to them after he retired from the first class game in 1979. A stockily built left hander, his batting was characterised by immense concentration, courage, patience, and defensive power. Yet he contrived always to push the score along. His style was not attractive; he would nudge, dab and deflect when the bowling was tight, but let anyone bowl him a hittable ball and his drive, pull or cut was struck with all the power of the sturdiest forearms of his generation.

When he retired, he had scored more runs – about 40,000 – than any other current player; reached a hundred hundreds; and taken more than 300 catches, many in the gully where he was alert and fearless. Briefly he captained Surrey but

Edrich drives Yuile for 6, England v. New Zealand, third Test, Headingley, 1965.

that coincided with an unsettled period in his career; he did not feel it a success and was happy to step down.

His 5,138 runs, at 43.54, in Tests record the defiance of a man who never wavered; was as firm as a rock in a losing side, sound in a winning one. Often he was the target of fast bowlers; notably in his last Test – the third against West Indies in 1976. He and his opening partner, Close – and there can never have been a more resistant pair in all cricket – were subjected to as savage a hammering by Holding, Roberts and Daniel as ever was seen on a cricket ground. They put on 54 for the first wicket in the last innings either ever played for England, and finished unbowed. That was typical of John Edrich; he is, as he looks, a steady, practical, honest, determined man; with all the Edrich courage.

Mike Procter

Prolonged observation of the overseas players who entered English cricket after the special registration legislation of 1968 divides them sharply into two groups. There are the mercenaries and the cricketers. Mike Procter could hardly ignore the financial advantages of his contract with Gloucestershire, but he has obviously enjoyed his cricket with them. Gloucestershire and English cricket, too, have enjoyed him. A most generous all-round cricketer, he has been an asset to the county game.

OPPOSITE TOP: Gloucestershire v. Lancashire, County Championship, Cheltenham, 1972.
OPPOSITE BOTTOM: Gloucestershire v. Hampshire, John Player League, Portsmouth, 1977.
ABOVE: Graeme Pollock, Hampshire v. South Africans, Southampton, 1965.

A volcanic fast bowler capable of turning a game within a few minutes, his action is not to be recommended as a model for young cricketers. From time to time the excesses of his apparently surprise delivery have limited the effectiveness of his technically unorthodox bowling: though when it comes off, it destroys the best of batsmen. On his best days, his expansive stroke play is hardly surpassed in the current game, and is much relished by his team and the spectators. He is a generous and inspiring county captain who, in recent years, has lifted Gloucestershire by their bootstrings to higher levels than their individual talents demanded.

Graeme Pollock

The rest of the cricket world has seen much less than it might have wished of one of the finest of post-war batsmen in Graeme Pollock, the polished but powerful South African left-hander.

He and his brother Peter, the fast bowler, both played for Eastern Province and their Test careers were ended by the banning of South Africa from the international arena.

At sixteen, Graeme Pollock became the youngest man to score a century in Currie Cup cricket; at nineteen, the youngest South African to make a double century in the first class game; in 1965, when he was twenty, the youngest cricketer to reach a thousand runs in Test cricket. In only 23 Tests, in six series, between the ages of nineteen and twenty-five, he scored 2,256 runs at the remarkable average of 60.97; and made them in brilliant fashion. In his only tour of England (1965) South Africa took the rubber when they beat England in the second – Trent Bridge – Test; the only one of the three-match series to be finished. In that game Graeme Pollock scored 125 out of 160 in 140 minutes; caught Titmus brilliantly at slip and, although not a regular bowler, on the last day he took the valuable wicket of M. J. K. Smith with a leg break. South Africa's greatest triumph, of course, was to win all four matches of the rubber – their last in Test cricket – against Australia in 1969-70. Graeme Pollock's scores were 49, 50, 274 (the highest score for South Africa in Tests; made in 417 minutes), 52, 87, 1 and 4. On that English visit of 1965, he made 122 in two hours against Sussex and in the Kent match, 203 not out with five sixes and 28 fours. That innings at Canterbury evoked local memories of Frank Woolley and Pollock, similarly tall, slim, and graceful is, indeed, cast in the same mould; a felicitous but powerful punisher of all kinds of bowling.

Barry Richards

Barry Richards is undoubtedly the most talented batsman of the 1960s and '70s. He could destroy an attack in minutes without seeming to try, saunter down the pitch to fast-medium bowling as if it were slow – or throw away his wicket out of boredom. It is sad that the splendour of his footwork – when he was bothered to move – his stroke play, improvisation and invention did not give him more pleasure than it did. He wrote a book to say how relieved he was to leave county cricket and his team-mates, and left England to display his immense ability for World Series Cricket.

His highest skills had, in fact, already been seen by many, for it sometimes seemed that he reserved his best performances for television. An innings against Lancashire, and another against Leicestershire, before the cameras in the John Player League, were sheer virtuoso performances. In the photograph here, he is, as the golfers say 'hitting from the inside out'. As can be seen from the position the wicketkeeper has taken, the ball was aimed outside the line of the leg stump but, probably because there was a packed on side field – or merely for some whim of his own – Richards decided to hit it through the covers.

His gifts were apparent when he came to England in 1963, barely eighteen, as captain of the South African Schools team, with his friend Mike Procter. The two spent a season with Gloucestershire and then went home, but returned to England in 1968 when Procter went back to Gloucestershire, Richards to Hampshire, for whom he scored 2,395 runs in his first season. Rising 23, he was already a high class batsman. He admitted, reasonably enough, to wanting financial rewards commensurate to his skill and, surely enough, when he played the season for 1970-1 for South Australia, with the inducement of a dollar a run, he scored 1538 runs (average 109.86), a seasons's aggregate exceeded there only by Bradman.

A useful off-spinner – he took seven for 63 against the 1968 Rest of the World side – and a natural slip fielder, he might have been an outstanding all-rounder. He felt, though, that batting was hard enough work and gave up bowling.

He has passed every examination, except – as one old player made the point very strongly – the perpetual attack of fast bowlers. Such bowlers concentrated, over the years, on battering such batsmen as Len Hutton, Colin Cowdrey, Ian and Greg Chappell, Geoffrey Boycott, Peter May and Ken Barrington into submission; all those batsmen handled the aggression well enough at the start, but gradually the perpetual concentrated high-standard hammering – not merely of Test class bowlers but of a *concentration* of Test fast bowlers – wore them down. Richards, in his four Tests – all against Australia – averaged 72.57: but he never had to face the long-term strain. No one who has not faced the ultimate, distasteful test has yet passed into the company of the great. That Rubicon has always been one of character, and there – never in the realm of talent – lies the doubt about Richard's qualification for greatness.

OPPOSITE: Richards drives a ball pitching outside his leg stump, Hants. v. Lancs., Gillette Cup, Bournemouth, 1972.

Sind XI, v. M.C.C.,
Karachi, 1978.

Mohsin Khan

In 1978 Pakistan, their main Test-playing strength having defected to the Packer World Series, brought to England an inexperienced side. Mohsin Khan was one of that team. A twenty-four-year-old with a Test career of a single match, at home he played for Habib Bank, but had been a professional for two seasons with Todmorden in the Lancashire League. He toured West Indies in 1976-7 without being chosen for a Test; and had his one representative innings against Brearley's side in Pakistan, when he scored 44. A slim, personable right-hander, he found himself in England a member of a team doomed to defeat.

The Pakistanis played below their potential and were beaten by an innings in the first two Tests while the third was left drawn in rain. In this tatterdemalion side – weakened as much by the failure of the main players who made the team as the loss of the Packer men – Mohsin batted with outstanding style and courage. His scores – and the totals in which they were made –

were 35 (out of 164), 38 (231), 31 (105), 46 (139), 41 (201); three times he was the highest scorer of the innings.

Upstanding in style, he had learnt more than a little of English conditions during his time in Lancashire. Of all the Pakistani batsmen he was the most cool, correct and relaxed, unflinching against pace, competent in dealing with movement off the pitch; and, at least twice in the Tests, extremely unlucky to be out. The release and return of seven Packer players – six of them batsmen – for the home series with India meant that, for reasons of 'face' and cricket politics, they all had to be included in every Test team. Thus two good innings for Young Pakistan and a century for Sind Province against the touring side were not enough to win Mohsin a place in that series. The impression remains from the 1978 tour to England, though, that he may be his country's outstanding batsman of the new generation.

Majid Khan

Majid Jehangir Khan is one of the few batsmen of our time who is touched with genius. A devout Muslim, strict teetotaller and non-smoker; barely heard to swear, even mildly, he is completely relaxed on the field – because his religious philosophy convinces him that a game should not be important enough to disturb a man. Originally a bowler – like his cousin Imran – of considerable pace, in his first Test he took the wickets of Bill Lawry, in both innings, and Brian Booth. His seam bowling career was ended by a back injury and, perhaps, some doubt about his action.

His father, Majid Jehangir Khan, was a Blue at Cambridge, where he was a contemporary of Wilfred Wooller, who as a result was able to persuade Majid, when he came down from University, to join Glamorgan. Jehangir, a history lecturer at Punjab University and a former Education Minister in West Pakistan, has concerned himself with cricket administration since he returned there; but to avoid any suggestion of nepotism he resigned from the board of selectors when Majid was chosen to play in a Test.

A most superb stroke-maker, yet without any flourish or flamboyance about his play, Majid, on his day, is as great a destroyer of bowling as either of the Richards. Equally strong off front foot or back, his play lit by a sharp intelligence, he can cut or glance delicately, or hit as hard as almost any contemporary player. Those who watched the televised match between Northamptonshire and Glamorgan at Wellingborough in 1975 will recall a quite striking dominance of the bowling as he scored the fastest fifty in the history of that competition – off only 22 balls – and went on to a chanceless 75 in 27 minutes with five sixes and seven fours.

Majid became one of the few non-Welshmen to be completely, even happily, accepted by the Glamorgan public; and in 1973 he took over the captaincy of the county in succession to Tony Lewis. In 1976, though, he first resigned from that office – declaring there had been interference with his captaincy – and then left the club. In 1974 he won the one day international against England at Trent Bridge virtually off his own bat with an apparently carefree but utterly masterly century in 28 overs. In some ways a cricketer for cricket's sake, he has played for Queensland in the Sheffield Shield, captained Pakistan, signed for World Series and, wherever he has gone, batted with an unstressed brilliance.

England v. Pakistan, third Test, The Oval, 1974.

Greg Chappell

Greg Chappell is a great batsman of natural grace and timing. His ability was early apparent and, during the absence of the national team on tour in South Africa in 1966-7, he was selected, eighteen years old, for South Australia in the Sheffield Shield and confirmed his selection with a century and two sixties. In 1968, still only nineteen, he joined Somerset as a student of the English game. Almost at once he scored the first century – in 88 minutes – ever made in the John Player League, and went on to make 128 (with 19 fours) out of 170. He scored over a thousand runs in each of his two Championship seasons; switched from his normal leg-breaks to mediumpace 'seam up' to conform to the English cricketing economy, and fielded superbly at cover point.

He made friends not merely by his cricket but by his manner and his manners; for, resistant as he could be as player and captain, he never showed the – half-assumed – raw aggression of his brother Ian. He enjoyed his period of study; but his Test-playing ambitions dictated that, after two seasons with Somerset, he should return to Australia. Surely enough, in the next year, he became one of the historic few who have scored a century in their first Test innings, with 108 to pull his side out of trouble against England at Perth. With the 1972 Australians, under his brother Ian, he made 131 at Lord's; and 113 at The Oval in an historic partnership when the two Chappells both made centuries in the same innings of the same Test, and put on 201 together.

The two set a record hardly likely to be beaten when, against New Zealand at Wellington, in 1973-4, they became the only two brothers each to score two centuries in the same Test. Greg's aggregate in that match, 380 (247 not out and 133) is a record for matches between the two countries. Against West Indies at Brisbane in 1975-6 he became the only man to score centuries in each innings of his first Test as captain. By these standards England hardly saw the best of this unquestionably great batsman, for he was less than fit when he came back to England in 1975. Although he never said as much for publication, he was dragged down by deep-seated and debilitating glandular fever and did not do himself justice; though he played an innings of determined courage to save the second Test, and the rubber, for Australia. In 1977 he was captain of a side riven by dissensions and unsettled by the Packer defections. Again and again he stood

Greg Chappell, Sussex v. Australians, Hove, 1977.

up like a rock in Australia's sea of defeat; and at
Lord's he scored his last Test century before
announcing his retirement from Test cricket.

Memory will always recall him, tall and slim,
echoing the words used of the Victorian batsman, Joseph Guy – 'All ease and elegance, fit to
play before the Queen in Her Majesty's parlour.'
Because of his steely wrists and innate sense of
timing, he was a superbly clean and powerful
driver; good, and good-looking, all round the
wicket but especially strong on the leg side, and
one of the rare batsmen to play the pure, classical
on drive. A quick-witted and clear-minded
captain, he had become a fine slip catcher in a
great close fielding combination. His retirement
at 29 was a tragic loss to the entire tradition and
history of cricket; but more than anyone else who
joined World Series Cricket, Greg Chappell did
so with dignity and with courtesy towards the
establishment game which had produced him.
He will, surely, return.

Ian Chappell

Australian cricket upheavals are generally
violent, and not always logical. Bill Lawry was
dropped for the final Test of 1970-1 because his
team had lost to England; despite the fact that he
averaged 40 in the series.

He was replaced by Ian Chappell, who was
defeated in his first, second and fourth matches
and then began a row of successes in which
Australia beat all comers. He added Thomson
and Walker to the maturing Lillee, and drilled as
good a cadre of close catchers as any side has ever
had. Batting against Australia became a
dangerous exercise. Chappell, though, did more
than change the playing strength; he altered the
character of Australian cricket. It became more
efficient, harder, tougher and more combative –
even belligerent. He turned his side into almost a
caricature of the Australian character. The Board
warned him for his side's use of foul langauge,
the 'protest' of the head-high 'beamer', and for
wearing a patent cricket boot with coloured
stripes. Chappell, a typical Australian in his
attitude to authority, did not hesitate to answer
back, nor to use the press to publicise his views.
He protested against the inadequacy of payments
to players and negotiated improved terms with
the Board. He was, above all, a players' player;
his friends were in the dressing room and on the
field; and he never got less than maximum effort
from them.

Grandson of Victor Richardson, brother of

Ian Chappell, Prudential World Cup Final, Lord's, 1975.

Greg and Trevor, he was a bred cricketer. As a
batsman he was almost wilfully unpolished; no
such stylist as his brother Greg, but a sturdy
opponent, grim in defence, militant in attack;
always ready to counter the fast bowler who
dropped short with a hook or, as he grew wiser, a
more controlled pull in front of square. Only four
Australians – Bradman, Harvey, Simpson and
Lawry – have scored more than his 4,738 runs in
Test cricket. He could bowl leg breaks with some
skill and was a first class slip field, sharp and
secure. A cricketer of effect rather than the
graces.

England v. Australia, third Test, Headingley, 1975.

Ross Edwards

It was characteristic of Ross Edwards that, in 1977, he was at 32 the oldest member of the Australian touring side in England, and its specialist cover point. One of the group who led Western Australia to its recent high standard of performance, Ross, rosy faced, enthusiastic and extremely fit, was a model team member. He was content to regard himself as a run of the mill cricketer. Yet, in 1972, sent in first in the second innings of the Trent Bridge Test because Bruce Francis was ill, he scored 170 not out in 330 minutes without the vestige of a chance. It was a well made innings, played in his characteristic upstanding fashion, straight in defence; its best scoring strokes those off the back foot, especially the cut. Sent in first in both innings of the next Test, he made a 'pair'. But he made local history at Perth in 1974 against England, when he became the first West Australian to score a Test century in his home state.

He averaged 40.37 an innings, with two centuries, in the 32 innings of his twenty Tests. A cheerful, intelligent man, and a competent accountant, he was one of the last victims of the Australian 'amateur' cricket economy. Returning from overseas tours to find himself out of work, he felt bound after the 1977 English visit to retire from the game in the interests of his family. Fortunately for him, after he had retired, there came the opportunity to earn some degree of compensation from Packer which, as he said, he could not afford to refuse.

He was always outstanding as a fieldsman, particularly in the covers, where his rapid judgment, balanced mobility, clean pick-up and accurate throwing saved many runs – especially when batsmen refused runs to him that they would have taken to lesser fieldsmen. To this end he kept himself so fit. Often when the fast bowlers were on, he was the only off side fieldsman in front of the wicket, with no one nearer on the on side than forward short leg. Then his speed and eagerness were to be seen as major assets in keeping the game tight. Ross Edwards was always good company, an honest, optimistic man, not a great cricketer, but a good one, who enjoyed his game and shared his pleasure.

Rodney Hogg

Rodney Hogg had one of the most unexpected entries into modern Test cricket. After four years of intermittent selection at Colts level in Victoria, he had not won a place in the State side. In 1975, he decided to move to South Australia. There he played three games in the 1975-6 Sheffield Shield but none in 1976-7. Described in the local press as a 'wild man', he was inclined to take a tilt at authority, and to bowl short to batsmen. When the 1978-9 season began he had taken 45 wickets (at 25.46) in 11 first class matches. After being a dental assistant in the army, an insurance agent, and out of work for a period ('My idea of life was to be rich and lazy, and play cricket') he had become a milk roundsman in Adelaide. Then, in the first week of November 1978, for South Australia against the English touring side, he took four for 43 and two for 39; including Boycott twice, Gooch, Radley – hit on the head and out of touch for the rest of the tour – and Miller. That took Hogg into the team for the first Test, where he took six for 74 and two for 35 (Gooch and Brearley twice each, Boycott, Botham, Miller and Edmonds). He was a genuine fast bowler who had brought his length, direction and – almost – his temperament under control, had developed the capacity to move the ball both ways, and lived down the theory that his asthmatic condition seriously impaired his stamina. The wickets he took were generally valuable; and, most usefully for Yallop, he had a consistently disturbing effect on Boycott and Brearley.

Ten wickets in the second Test; another ten, which virtually won the third and put Australia back into the contest; six on a spinner's wicket in the fourth; seven in the fifth and he had beaten Arthur Mailey's fifty-eight-year-old Australian record of 36 wickets in a series against England. By the end of the six match rubber he had lifted the figure to 41: a phenomenally rapid rise to eminence, even by Australian standards.

Hogg shows the occasional ability to fall over after a delivery, Australia v. England, second Test, Perth, 1978-9.

Max Walker,
England v.
Australia, second
Test, Old Trafford,
1977.

RIGHT: Rodney
Marsh, England v.
Australia, third
Test, Headingley,
1975.

Max Walker

A tall and powerfully-built fast-medium bowler, Max Walker was a key member of the highly successful Australian pace attack under Ian Chappell in, especially, 1974-5 in Australia and 1975 in England. His speed was not so high as that of Lillee or Thomson but crucially he maintained pressure while they rested. Thus, in the six-match series of 1974-5, they took 81 of the wickets that fell to Australian bowlers and Walker's share was 23. In England in the following summer he had 14 (including seven in the decisive first Test) of the 51 taken by the three out of 75 altogether. He was never quite so successful in England as in Australia because his was essentially an Australian length, importantly shorter than that generally employed by his kind in this country. His stamina, though, was never in question; with bustling approach and whirling action he was accurate enough to keep most batsmen in check and was regarded by colleagues and opponents as an unlucky bowler.

In 1972-3, early in his Test career, he had figures of six for 15 against Pakistan at Sydney; and went on to take 26 wickets in the series in West Indies. He proved a useful batsman against England on his home pitches in 1974-5 when he averaged 44.20 and constantly set up valuable tail-end resistance. When he joined W.S.C. he had taken 138 wickets in his 43 Tests.

A native of Tasmania, he emigrated to Melbourne, and his main cricket career has been with Victoria. His fine physique, shock of dark hair and luxuriant moustache make him a striking figure: he is an architect by profession; an extremely good-natured person, and a superb raconteur.

Rodney Marsh

Rodney Marsh, the Australian wicketkeeper of the Chappell era, is an aggressive cricketer. Originally a poor catcher of the ball, he became, for all his heavy build, a fine acrobatic wicketkeeper by any standard except that of style. He stands first among Australian wicketkeepers with 198 dismissals (190 catches and eight stumpings) in only 52 Tests. Brother of the international golfer, Graham Marsh, his understanding of the difference between the financial returns of the two games was an important ingredient of the Australian cricketers' discontent which finally erupted in the shift to W.S.C. Marsh is less aggressive than his behaviour often suggests. There is a certain bearish

humour in his reactions to opponents and events. His expression, as in this picture, of exasperation at someone – in this case Keith Fletcher – constantly playing and missing at Lillee – is not calculated to reinforce the batsman's confidence. A stern competitor; a powerful left hand bat – the first Australian wicketkeeper to score a Test century – Marsh strove, usually successfully, to conceal a romantic attachment to cricket.

Dennis Lillee,
England v.
Australia, third,
Test, Headingley,
1975.

RIGHT: Jeff
Thomson, a
Middlesex XI v.
Australians,
Lord's, 1975.

Dennis Lillee

Dennis Lillee is, by any standard of any period, an outstanding fast bowler. He is remarkable if not unique, in coming back to bowl truly fast after a severe spinal injury. His pace has always been high but he sharpened his attack by subtle variations; the use of the bouncer – aimed, he said, at the rib cage, but also often at the head – the yorker, fierce outswing and controlled changes of pace. Few fast bowlers have had finer physique or technique, or such a gloriously flowing action. He added edge to it; with a hostility to his opponents often theatrical and sometimes offensive. He would have been greater still without that.

Jeff Thomson

Jeff Thomson is a splendidly fast bowler of the explosive type. While most men of high pace build up their delivery speed by a long run, Thomson takes only a short approach and then uses an immensely violent, circular, delivery heave. A hostile cricketer, he bowls one of the most disconcerting bouncers of an age which has devoted much attention to that tactic. His performance has not been even, and he has been often handicapped by injury, but he effectively won several Tests; and he probably never bowled better in his life than for Australia against West Indies at Bridgetown, Barbados in 1977-8. He had made the tour reluctantly, resenting even his availability; his inclinations leaning towards the Packer W.S.C. operation, but his contractual obligations to a radio station compelling him to stay temporarily with the establishment game. Nevertheless he produced a magnificently sustained operation of high pace to cut open the West Indian batting with six for 77.

Eventually, a court action brought by the Australian Board delayed his joining W.S.C. by a few months; but he went to them by the start of their 1978-9 season. A constantly controversial figure, by no means always judicious in his public utterances and gestures, he was, at his best, a spectacular and devastating fast bowler. In three series, spread over four years, he formed with Lillee a fast-bowling pairing which, directed by Ian Chappell, backed by that magnificent close-fielding posse, and with the steady Walker in support, must rank with any cricket has known.

England v. West Indies, Trent Bridge, first Test, 1976.

Vivian Richards

There is no more exciting batsman in modern cricket than Vivian Richards. Pleasure in playing with or against him, or watching him, is heightened by his own obvious joy in playing cricket, and especially batting. Like Andy Roberts, the fast bowler of Hampshire and West Indies, Richards comes from Antigua. Indeed, they travelled to England together in 1973, financed by local subscription, to seek their fortunes at cricket through Alf Gover and his school.

Still Richards had no worthwhile record – not even a century in a first class match – when the West Indian selectors imaginatively preferred him to the infinitely more experienced Rohan Kanhai for their 1974-5 tour of India and Pakistan. There he scored 370 Test runs; and, with 829 in four games against England, set a record for a calendar year in 1976 when, in the course of 11 Tests, he made 1,710 runs.

Compactly built, lithe, amazingly quick in assessment, fast on his feet, he has virtually all the classic strokes and invents others. A joyous player, he sometimes seems almost intoxicated by the headiness of his own stroke-play, so that he throws away his wicket. Since he came to

Somerset in 1974 he had barely known failure until their unhappy weekend in September 1978 when they lost the Gillette Cup Final on the Saturday and the John Player League – which they were also expected to win – on the Sunday. There can be no doubt that Viv Richards did not succeed in those two matches because he was trying too hard. He was obviously so committed that he played with unaccustomed doggedness, rather than risk failure. He almost succeeded but, in the end, his sense of duty prevented him from batting like himself. Normally he takes cricket as a game, and can even laugh when he is out; but not then – he did not so much fear to fail as a batsman as to fail his team mates.

His speed of reaction makes him a fine fieldsman anywhere – with three early run outs he tilted the first World Cup final to the West Indies – and he is delighted when he takes wickets with his off breaks. No imported player has ever been more popular in Somerset; and the quality of his stroke play is such that few have ever given such splendid entertainment. He bats like a happy millionaire; and Somerset could not bear to part with him.

h, Somerset v. Australians,
7. Jeff Thomson.

The Oval, England v.
Australia, fourth Test,
1975. Dennis Lillee.

Garfield Sobers

The game of cricket has never known a more versatile nor more effective all-round cricketer than Garfield Sobers. He began as an orthodox slow left-arm bowler; developed wrist spin until he was a commanding and baffling practitioner of the 'Chinaman'; and then, to meet Frank Worrell's tactical need, became a most effective fast-medium left-arm bowler with a spontaneous, ideal action. A self-taught left-hander, he batted like a prince, free, without flaws in defence, a generous maker of strokes, a fearless hooker of the short ball; a delicate cutter or imperious driver of spin. Marvellously athletic in the covers, he was a bewilderingly sharp short leg to the off spin of Lance Gibbs; or a peerless slip to his fast bowlers. There can be little doubt that if he had wished he could have been an international wicketkeeper. As a captain, he was not forgiven by some captious critics for losing a Test match – against England at Port-of-Spain in 1967-8 when he declared in the attempt to force a win after three draws. The effort by which he almost won the following match off his own bat is an epic all too rarely recounted. With scores of 152 and 95 not out, and three wickets in each innings, he failed by only one wicket.

His 8,032 runs for West Indies is the highest individual aggregate in Test cricket: while he took 235 wickets and made 110 catches.

He eventually wearied of the captaincy, and jet travel exposed him to the intolerable strain of twelve-month-a-year cricket for Barbados, West Indies, Nottinghamshire, South Australia, International Cavaliers and in the Leagues. Garfield Sobers was, beyond all question, the most brilliant all-round cricketer: but sheer hard labour broke him. He hobbled round England on his farewell circuit of the crowds he had delighted – and who bade him the warmest and most grateful goodbyes.

LEFT: England v.
West Indies,
second Test,
Edgbaston, 1973.

England v. West
Indies, first Test,
The Oval, 1973.

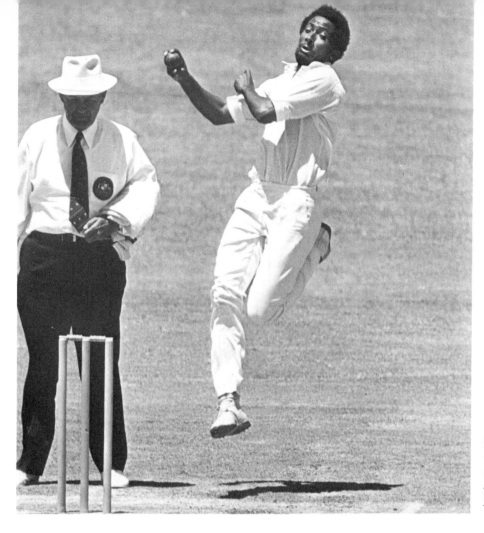

Andy Roberts took 7 for 54, his best Test match performance, Australia v. West Indies, second Test, Perth, 1975-6.

Andy Roberts

Andy Roberts, the fast bowler from Antigua, made an immense early impact on first class and county cricket. When he joined Hampshire in 1973 he had not commanded a regular place in the Combined Islands side. After a qualifying season with Hampshire's second XI, he was summoned back to West Indies for the 1973-4 series but played only a single Test against England and then was dropped. In England during the following summer, though, he was the first bowler to 100 wickets and ended the season top of the first class averages. Chosen for the tours of 1974-5 in India–Pakistan; 1975-6 in Australia, England in 1976 and the home series of 1976-7 with Pakistan, he took his first hundred wickets in Test cricket in the record time of 2 years 144 days. In fact, if he had not played in that isolated 1974 Test, his record would have been all but unapproachable – under two years.

That spell of success, though, impaired his quality. Until then, a spare six feet two, physically able to relax when not bowling; having a smooth approach and a strong sinewy body, he seemed undistressed by bowling. He preferred short, forty-minute spells and hour-long rests but the temptation was always there to keep him on. He was the sharpest cutting edge either his county or his Test captain could command; and, even when he was not taking wickets, he was economical.

At his best, Roberts' pace was blistering; his tactics shrewd; his control immaculate. After 1976, he began to suffer injuries and strains; and he was never again able to shoulder comparable stints. He is still, in brief spells, one of the finest fast bowlers in the world; but he tires more easily – and returns more reluctantly – than of old. Those who saw him bowl between 1974 and 1976, though, have no doubt that he was an eminent fast bowler.

John Shepherd

There is a considerable difference, which is not always recognised, between the two types of overseas cricketers in the English game. There are those who were imported as established stars – like Rohan Kanhai, Clive Lloyd, Asif Iqbal, Farouk Engineer, Wayne Daniel – and those, such as John Shepherd, who arrived in England as promising young players and eventually graduated to the high level of performance while they were playing with English counties.

Colin Cowdrey and Leslie Ames saw John Shepherd in Barbados before he even played first class cricket, and invited him to come over and play with Kent second XI. In fact he won a county cap there in 1967 and in the following winter, back in West Indies with hope of winning a Test place, he top-edged a bouncer into his face, fractured a cheekbone and lost much cricket time and some confidence from the injury.

In 1968 in England, when he missed the all-rounder's double by only four wickets, he played a major part in helping Kent to second place in the Championship. In the next summer he became a Test all-rounder for West Indies in England. At Old Trafford he bowled as steadily as a clock, 58 overs to take five for 104; and played twice against India in West Indies in 1970-1, but after that, he and West Indian authority did not see eye to eye.

The Rhodesians and South Africans were happy about his visits to play in their countries but West Indians were not. He was enjoyed, too, in Australia where he has played grade cricket for Footscray in Melbourne.

A cheerful, friendly man, he is preponderantly a front foot batsman with considerable hitting power (four sixes in an over against Somerset at Canterbury); a medium pace bowler of tight control and immense variety of swing, cut and pace changes. As a fieldsman he challenges even Alan Ealham as a safe catcher close to the wicket or in the country. Lissom, a smooth mover, and essentially sure-handed, he gathers the ball and returns at a speed which compels respect.

John Shepherd at extra cover, Kent v. Lancashire, Gillette Cup Final, Lord's, 1974.

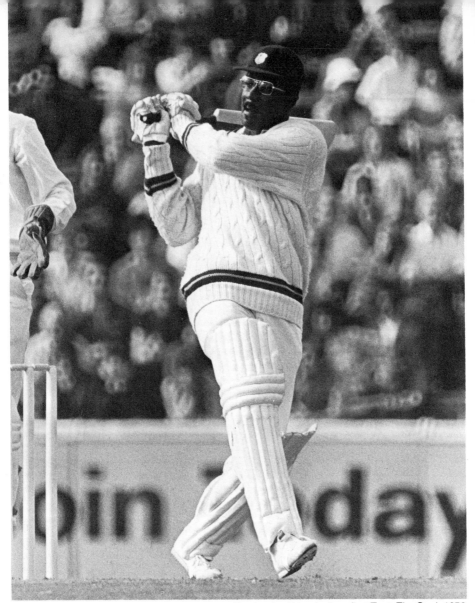

England v. West Indies, first Test, The Oval, 1973.

Clive Lloyd

A strong link in the remarkable, and apparently unending, chain of brilliant West Indians is Clive Lloyd, from Guyana, who went to play for Haslingden in the Lancashire League, joined Lancashire and became one of the most entertaining cricketers in the world. Even for one of his considerable height – six feet five inches – his arms are disproportionately long; and he uses an unusually heavy bat. Add great strength of biceps and shoulders, and an uninhibited swing, and he is explicably one of the hardest hitters the game has ever known. Only a few seasons ago, from a wicket pitched on the gasometer side of The Oval, he levered a fast medium bowler out of the ground to the wall of Archbishop Tenison

School on the other side of Harleyford Road.

For a match-winning scorer of quick runs, he has the impressive average in all first class cricket of almost fifty; and of 43.35 in 63 Tests; while he is a superb fieldsman. Originally a leg spin bowler, he switched to accurate, medium pace, 'seam up' to meet the demands of the league and one-day game. Relaxed, modest, quietly spoken and likeable, he is a sympathetic captain of West Indies; but deeply concerned about the poor financial rewards for players in that country. When Lancashire engaged Lloyd and Farouk Engineer in 1968 they laid the foundation of their success as a one-day cricketing side. Lloyd, steady bowler, attacking bats-

Clive Lloyd throws in, Australia v. West Indies, first Test, Brisbane, 1975-6.

man and great fieldsman anywhere, was ideally suited to that form of the game. Accepted happily into the side, he has made many friends in Lancashire and in cricket; and among spectators everywhere.

Through the generations a series of cover points have been voted the finest the game has known – Vernon Royle, Gilbert Jessop, Jack Hobbs, Albert Slater, Cyril Washbrook, Reggie Simpson, Gul Mahommad, Paul Sheahan, Colin Bland. Few of them, if any, can have been finer than Clive Lloyd. As he slouched, round shouldered, at cover or in over-limit play anywhere in the deepfield, he gave no suggestion of his quality. Once the ball was played anywhere

near him, though, he reacted like some huge cat. If the well-struck ball seemed to be passing wide of him, he would hurl his great length far and fast like a soccer goalkeeper to make the stop and, before he even got to his feet, would, with a twist of the body, throw the ball a remarkable distance for a recumbent man. Let him reach it on his feet and his gather took the ball in a throwing position – no need to draw back his arm – and the throw was flat, fast and deadly. He achieved enough run outs to make the batsmen of six countries – including his own – think twice – nay, four times – about taking a single to him.

Barbados v. Australians, Bridgetown, 1978.

Wayne Daniel

Wayne Daniel toured England with the West Indian schoolboys team of 1974. Two years later he was back again as the youngest of the three West Indian fast bowlers – the other two were Roberts and Holding – who routed the English batting and won the Test rubber by three to none. As the junior of the combination he took only thirteen wickets in his four Tests. He was, though, clearly a considerable bowler with an admirable temperament. Of mighty physique for a twenty-year-old, conscientiously fit and with great stamina, he needed to rationalise his action and he did so convincingly. In 1977, still only twenty-one, he became qualified for Middlesex where he promised to last longer than Holding or Roberts and to be a major asset for some years to come.

Glenn Turner

Glenn Turner is one of the few New Zealanders who may be described as a world class batsman. He has much natural ability, but he has never relied upon it; rather, he set out to make himself a batsman.

He was seventeen, and still at school – where he had an awe-inspiring record – when he was first picked for Otago. Two years later, Billy Ibadulla, formerly of Warwickshire, who had settled in New Zealand as a coach, undertook to send him to Edgbaston for a trial. Thereupon Turner gave up his job in insurance to work night shifts in a bakery to pay his fare. Before he could set off, Warwickshire wrote to say that they already had their full quota of overseas players, but would honour their pledge of a trial and, if possible, recommend him to another county. It was more than possible: as soon as they saw him bat in the nets, they listed a sequence of five counties. The first to see him – Worcestershire – signed him at once. He spent his qualifying year of 1967 in the second XI, was given a first team place and his cap in 1968.

The next year he promptly joined the New Zealand touring team in England and, in the Lord's Test, went in first and carried his bat through the innings. On to his first Test century on New Zealand's Pakistan tour, from which he returned a fully rounded player, able to think out, plan and build an innings, not coming by runs, but positively making them. That year also saw him beat the Worcestershire record of C.F. Walters with ten centuries in a county season. He had made nine when, in the county's last fixture but one – against Lancashire – he was run out by the solitary off side fieldsman – of course, it was Clive Lloyd – for 99. In the last match, though, in full command psychologically and technically, he scored the tenth – ironically enough, against Warwickshire. In a phenomenal burst of scoring on the New Zealand tour of West Indies in 1971-2, he scored four double centuries – two in Tests – and had an average of 96.00 for the series. In 1973 he became the only batsman since 1938 to achieve the feat – which had been described as 'impossible now' – of scoring 1,000 runs in May. Already it is possible to say that, of all Worcestershire batsmen, only Tom Graveney, or, perhaps, briefly, Cyril Walters, was better than Glenn Turner. He has already outscored Walters, and his runs – he remains greedy for them – may yet outweigh Graveney's.

Glenn Turner scoring his 1000th run, Northants. v. New Zealanders, Northants, 31st May, 1973.

Bhagwat Chandrasekhar

Bhagwat Chandrasekhar – known in India and on the cricket grounds of five countries as 'Chandra' – is, after Richie Benaud and Clarrie Grimmett, the most successful wrist spinner in all Test cricket. He has taken 241 wickets at 29.12 (April, 1979). In common with most of his kind, he has not been consistent, but, on his day, he has won matches at the highest level: historically, when he took eight for 114 at The Oval in 1971 to give India their first win over England in England; and 12 for 104 at Melbourne in 1977-8 to bring about their first in Australia.

An attack of poliomyelitis when he was five left him with a withered right arm which he believes – by its flexible thinness – gives him the whippy action which makes his bowling so effective. Chandra is tall and lean and vibrant; essentially an attacking bowler. His pace is unusually brisk for a wrist spinner and, if he bowls relatively few leg-breaks – they are frequent enough to make it a bad batting bet to say that he never does – he traffics generally in a bounding top spinner and the googly. These – as distinct from the leg-break (which is usually employed to gain an off side catch) – are aimed at the stumps and, thus, Chandra takes most of his wickets bowled or LBW; especially on hard pitches where he makes the ball hurry through.

Chandrasekhar bowls to Zaheer Abbas, Pakistan v. India, second Test, Lahore, 1978.

Bishen Singh Bedi

Bishen Singh Bedi, one of the great practitioners in the classical fashion of finger spin, has taken more Test wickets than any other slow left arm bowler. Derek Underwood, who is ahead of him, is not true slow left arm, but a phenomenon; a medium paced spinner.

Bedi, the artistic philosopher, had no coaching as a bowler. He simply rolled a cricket ball out of his fingers and quite naturally developed the most easily rhythmical action it is possible to conceive. He uses precisely the same weapons of attack as Wilfred Rhodes, flight, spin, variation of length, patience and understanding of bats-

men. The faster ball, a floater, one which goes with the arm, and differing degrees of spin, are all phases of a pattern of subtle variations intended to persuade the batsman to destroy himself. When Northants decided to dispense with the services of Bishen Bedi at the end of the 1977 season, they made a comment upon modern English cricket. Slow wickets, and the fact that the over-limit game has elevated the brief 'slog' above the built innings have combined to sacrifice the spin bowler to crudity. That is not their fault; it certainly is not Bishen Bedi's. He remains a great bowler.

Farouk Engineer

The number of cricketers who find the competitive game fun grows smaller every year. One of the last of whom that was true was Farouk Engineer, the Indian Test wicketkeeper-batsman who played for Lancashire. Indian cricketers do not often find the game amusing; and that may be why Engineer was once dropped from an Indian Test team at a time when he was unquestionably not only the best wicketkeeper-batsman they had, but the best wicketkeeper. Ebullient, extrovert, bubbling with humour and enjoyment, he returned from one of his spells of selectorial disfavour to score 94 before lunch off the West Indian fast bowlers. As an attacking

Tony Greig and Farouk Engineer in collision, England v. India, first Test, Old Trafford, 1974.

batsman, he was capable of collaring and demoralising an opposing attack – or of throwing away his wicket by some extravagant gesture. Entitled to a place in any side as a wicketkeeper, he was equally worth it as a batsman in the over-limit game. With Clive Lloyd he gave Jack Bond the streak of aggression in batting needed for Lancashire's success in one-day play. A friendly, gregarious, generous man, busiest of cricketers, he had a prehensile catching ability; and he was, all the time, a cheerful but determined aggressor in the field; altogether a relishable cricketer.

Three Yorkshire Centurians

After Geoffrey Boycott completed his hundredth century in the Headingley Test of 1977, the photographers needed, and Yorkshire provided, a group of the three Yorkshire batsmen who had recorded a hundred hundreds. The senior was Herbert Sutcliffe from Gummerbridge; the imperturbable punitive hooker, and partner of Jack Hobbs in the greatest of all opening pairs.

The second, Len Hutton, who came from the edge of Pudsey; in 1938 against Australia at The Oval he set the towering Test record innings of 365. Finally Boycott, from Fitzwilliam, back in the England team and justified, could talk calmly about the level of achievement the three Yorkshiremen had attained.

Fred Trueman at point of delivery, Yorkshire v. Middlesex, Scarborough, 1965.

Fred Trueman

Fred Trueman was the archetypal Yorkshire fast bowler. Perfectly physically equipped for the task – wide-shouldered, thick necked, deep chested, heavy-hipped, strong-legged and solid-footed – he had a naturally perfect action. His ambition was simply to be a Yorkshire fast bowler. He had his setbacks; some, but by no means all, of his own creation. If he had his differences with authority, and once had a reputation as a rebel, he never stepped too far from the establishment line; and, his playing days over, he became, unopposed, a member of the Yorkshire club committee.

Between 1949 as an eighteen-year-old miner, and 1969 as an elder cricketer, he took 2,304 wickets at the unusually low average of 18.29; only five men took as many more cheaply; and, for prodigiously good measure, in the course of 67 Tests – spread over a period when he might have played in forty more – he took 307 wickets. That is substantially more than any other

English cricketer (though Underwood might still surpass the figure and, again, Trueman's rate was a most reasonable 21.57).

Fred looked a fast bowler; he sounded like a fast bowler; and he was a fast bowler. He commanded a savage late outswinger; sometimes made the ball come back off the pitch; had a deadly yorker; a well-hidden slower ball, and a bouncer which he sometimes overdid to the disadvantage of his figures and his side. In 1952, all cricketing England hailed him as the fast bowling retort to the Australians Lindwall and Miller; and, for more than a decade, he did his utmost to prove them right.

He could bat orthodoxly at a pinch, but he preferred to hit and sometimes did so spectacularly. He was, too, in his early days, a splendid – and startlingly ambidextrous – deepfielder, and later a Test standard short leg. He enjoyed it all, and ended up on the right side.

Jim Laker, 1977.

Jim Laker

Precise superlatives are rarely possible in cricket. The best batsman, best bowler, fastest bowler, best googly bowler, best wicketkeeper is a matter of opinion or dispute. It must, though, be possible to say that Jim Laker was the finest off-break bowler in the history of the game. Basically he spun the ball prodigiously. During the war, cricketers returning on leave from the North African theatre spoke with some awe of the off-spinner who gave the ball such a tweak that the non-striker heard it buzz as it passed his ear.

During Laker's teens in the Bradford area, Yorkshire, with characteristic thoroughness, had noted him as a promising young batsman; and he had some success with Saltaire in the Bradford Lague. When he returned to England after the war, he no longer had family reasons to go back to Yorkshire. He settled in the London area, joined Surrey and, at a stride, moved into county cricket as an off-spinner. Because he was so obviously gifted, too much was expected of him too soon; and the killer batsmen of the 1948 Australian side ruthlessly cut him down to size – especially in the Leeds Test which they won against the odds. He was too competitive a cricketer to surrender. He went back to the basics of his craft; control and variation of line, length, flight, pace, turn: he mastered it all. He could beat a batsman through the air or off the pitch; he was a conscious and conscientious craftsman. It was, though, five years before he could take on the Australians with the certainty of beating them: eight before he exacted his revenge for Headingly 1948.

In 1956 he achieved his prodigious performances of all ten wickets for Surrey against the Australians and nineteen in a Test against Australia at Old Trafford. That last feat was not performed on a consistently difficult pitch. It is not always recalled that there was a long period over the last three days when Colin McDonald, especially, demonstrated that it was perfectly possible to play Laker in these conditions. It is a measure of his distinction that he took the nineteen and won the match. His 46 wickets in that Test series is beaten only by S. F. Barnes who could not, however, better his average of 9.6.

A capable, correct batsman and a nimble gully field; he might have continued to bowl, long after his retirement, with the kind of advantage he demonstrated when he 'murdered' University batsmen in Sunday afternoon matches. He spent a couple of seasons as an emeritus spinner with Essex but then decided he had had enough; he was not prepared to be less than the best of his kind.

Frank Woolley

Frank Woolley probably was – and Sir Neville Cardus placed the claim beyond argument – the most felicitous of all batsmen. A tall, slim, left-hander who made the most elegant, yet heady, strokes against fast bowlers, he beguiled many years of inter-war spectators, especially at Canterbury. It is too easy for those who watched him then to forget that, in the years before the First World War, he was a true all-rounder who shared with Colin Blythe the morbid duty of destroying Kent's opponents on sticky wickets.

In that skill Blythe rendered Woolley much unselfish assistance which gave him – by virtue of his greater batting ability – the place Blythe might have had in the England side before the First World War. Especially that was so during the Triangular Tournament of 1912, when Woolley's slow left arm effectively won two crucial matches. He was, too, a magnificent slip whose tally of catches – 1,015 – is greater than that of anyone else except wicketkeepers.

Handsome in appearance as in batting style, he remained remarkably well-preserved, tall, slim, erect, silver-haired, rosy-cheeked and dignified until the last time he was seen, shortly before his death in 1978 at the age of 91.

Frank Woolley, 1965.

Lillee, Bradman
and Larwood at a
reception,
Centenary Test,
1977.

RIGHT:
Clarrie Grimmett,
1974.

Donald Bradman and Harold Larwood

The Centenary Test produced an historic meeting between Donald Bradman and Harold Larwood. (It was Alec Bedser who asserted 'the last bowler to be knighted was Sir Francis Drake'.) Bradman – 'The Don' – has been described by many who played with – and against – him as the greatest of all batsmen. Statistically it is difficult indeed to dispute the standing of a man who throughout his career averaged 95.14; and scored a century in one of every three innings he played. In Test cricket, his average was 99.4 an innings, and his incidence of centuries one in 1.8 matches. Neat, compactly built, with strong shoulders, quick on his feet, he was the most merciless punisher of even the marginally loose ball. As a boy he practised batting for hours by throwing a golf ball at a brick wall and, as it

rebounded, hitting it back with a small cricket stump. After that, bringing the middle of a cricket bat to a cricket ball was child's play. He perfected his fielding by throwing a golf ball at a single rounded fencing post and gathering the rebound: if he missed the post – or hit the wrong face on it – he had to retrieve the ball. He was the most efficient of all run-scorers; and subsequently an enlightened administrator of Australian cricket.

Harold Larwood was the Nottinghamshire coal-miner, hailed up from the pit in the traditional method of Derbyshire and Nottinghamshire when either county needed a fast bowler. Short by the standards of most of his kind, he had wide shoulders, deep chest, long arms and considerable wiry strength, and was

Clarrie Grimmett

Clarrie Grimmett, the Australian leg spinner, had the remarkable Test record of 216 wickets taken in only 37 matches. This is a frequency of almost six a match, which is paralleled only by his comrade in arms, Bill O'Reilly. Together they formed the most consistently destructive pair of spin bowlers in all Test cricket apart from Valentine and Ramadhin in 1950. Grimmett, short, spare and unobtrusive, bowled his leg breaks, googlies and – importantly – his 'flipper' or top spinner, with a low, almost round-arm action. He gave the batsman little rest, moving quickly in to bowl off his short run as soon as the ball was returned to him. He was remarkably accurate for a leg spinner and, psychologically artful, he out-witted many batsmen by his sudden variations of length within his patter-patter attack. He was born in New Zealand and entered the first-class game – with South Australia – quite late by Australian standards. Indeed some said, with fair reason, that he was older than his admitted 33 when he came into Test cricket and took eleven for 82 in his first match.

undoubtedly the fastest bowler in the world of his time. Douglas Jardine took him to Australia in 1932-3 to destroy Australia – which meant Bradman – by the leg theory tactic which Australians were to christen Body-line. Larwood and his county mate, Bill Voce, bowled short on the line of the body to a close leg side field and took The Ashes from Australia for the only time in the Bradman period of 1930-48. Statistically they reduced Bradman's average to 56.57; but that was enough. Otherwise he dominated cricket between the two countries for almost twenty years. Harold Larwood's career was shortened by injury and cricket politics; he remains, however, a legendary figure as the only bowler who ever effectively checked the progress of Sir Donald Bradman.

Centenary Celebrations

The Centenary Test celebrations of 1977 in Melbourne were the concept of Hans Ebeling. He was a fast-medium bowler for Victoria who made the 1934 tour to England and played his only Test, at The Oval, in that series. As an organiser of cricket's most important anniversary he was imaginative, efficient and – in terms of response, weather and the play – as fortunate as he deserved to be.

The idea was to bring to Melbourne for the Centenary match between England and Australia every living man who had ever played in an England–Australia Test in that country. Some – Herbert Sutcliffe, Frank Woolley and, the oldest Englishman, 'Tiger' Smith – reluctantly declared themselves too old to make the journey. Never-theless, some were able to accept the invitation to join the greatest gathering of Test cricketers in history. Among them was Jack Ryder, former Victorian and Australian all-rounder, captain and selector, who fell ill only two days after the celebrations, and died.

The cumulative effect of all these men under the same roof, lunching, dining, watching the play, reminiscing, recalling old triumphs – and failures – renewing acquaintances across forty or fifty years, produced an atmosphere of almost unbelievable nostalgia. It was an historic triumph and, on a human level, unforgettably reassuring and stimulating for some fine cricketers who had thought themselves forgotten.

Eddie Paynter

Eddie Paynter has become an almost legendary figure as the man who rose from a sickbed to play an innings which turned, and probably won, a Test match. At Brisbane in the 1932-3 series, Paynter was taken from the ground to hospital, suffering from tonsilitis. When he heard that English wickets were falling, he insisted, despite a high temperature, on going down to the Woolloongabba where England were 216 for six (Australia had made 340) when he went in. Last out, his 83, with the support of the tail, had helped England to 356. In the second innings he made the winning hit – a six – that won not only the match, but The Ashes.

It is historically revealing that such was the extent of the talent available to Lancashire at that time that, although Paynter joined their staff in 1920, he had to wait eleven years before he gained a regular first team place – at the age of thirty. Immediately he scored his first century – against Warwickshire at Old Trafford – and in the same year was picked for his first Test, against New Zealand, also at Old Trafford.

He became an accomplished batsman and brilliant fieldsman despite the loss of the tops of the first and second fingers of his right hand in an accident. A neat, quick-footed left-hander, he hit, as the boxers say, much more than his weight. He was strong all round the wicket; with cuts, hooks, pulls and drives. A joyous, lively, highly accomplished batsman and a naturally aggressive stroke-maker, he was hard to contain. In a bare twenty Tests he scored 1,540 runs at the rarely high average of 59.23: he must be ranked

Eddie Paynter, 1977.

OPPOSITE TOP:
Godfrey Evans (centre) en route to Melbourne, 1977.
OPPOSITE: Percy Fender with his grandson, 1977.

among the most unlucky of English cricketers that his first class career, delayed by Lancashire's wealth of talent, should have been ended by the outbreak of war.

No one enjoyed the Centenary Test celebrations more than Eddie Paynter. His brown eyes alive with memory and enjoyment, he could not speak warmly enough of the local Lancashire testimonial that paid for his travel to and from London and his hotels there, to enable him to make the trip. His delight was transparent; indeed, moving. The game never paid him a good wage; he had had his problems. When he died, all too soon afterwards, his friends realised the more warmly what a great compensation the centenary visit had been for his misfortunes.

Godfrey Evans

Godfrey Evans, the Kent and England wicket-keeper, was the ultimate cricketing extrovert. A professional boxer who gave up that career to concentrate on cricket, he was always a splendid competitor. His record of 219 dismissals – 173 catches and 46 stumpings – in the course of his 91 Test matches, has been overtaken by Alan Knott; but Evans' figures included such wide leg side catches as virtually established a fresh category of

the 'chance' to the wicketkeeper. Against West Indies, on an impossible wicket at Old Trafford in 1950, he scored the only hundred of the match to turn the game towards England (their only win of the series). He provided, too, a splendid psychological fillip to the rest of a team in the field.

A cheerful, friendly and convivial person, after his retirement Evans was, in turn, hotelier, publican, journalist, bookmaker's representative and public relations executive. All this time he was turning out in odd charity and benefit matches, demonstrating that his wicketkeeping – especially his ability to collect far distant catches – showed little decline.

Percy Fender

Percy George Fender was the oldest English cricketer to make the journey to the Centenary Test. He was 28 when he set out on the M.C.C.

Australian tour of 1920-1: 84 when he returned for the Melbourne celebrations. In the long interim his eyesight had failed and he was accompanied by his grandson who, he explained, 'is now my eyes'.

Percy George, as he was called, was an astute all-rounder and captain of Surrey. A spectacular hitter, his 100 against Northamptonshire in 35 minutes remains the fastest century ever scored in first class cricket. As he explained, it could have been faster if he had not waited for his partner to reach 200 before the captain declared. Fender was, too, a skilful bowler of wrist spin and various experiments; and by use of his wits he took many wickets on the batsmen's pitches at The Oval in the inter-war period. Add the fact that he was a certain slip catcher and a thoughtful strategist and you have, in Percy George Fender, one of the best all-round cricketers of the nineteen-twenties and early thirties.

Note on Photography

Cricket photography is largely an exercise in the use of long focus lenses. Cricket is unusual amongst sports in that the action invariably takes place along way from the spectator and the photographer.

All the photographs in this book were taken on the 35 mm format. I do not use the larger sizes, simply because the bigger the negative, the longer the lens you have to use. Even with 35 mm my equipment weighs as much as I am prepared to carry. I have always felt with careful processing and printing 35 mm can give a quality that is more than adequate for the printed page. The design of modern cameras and lenses is now of such a high standard that the weakest link in the chain towards the goal of quality is often the photographer himself.

For action photographs I use Nikon cameras, both the F2 and the FE. For a Test match in England I would use six bodies, all motor driven and loaded with a number of different films. For black and white these would be Ilford HP5 (rated at 400 ASA) and Kodak TRI-X (rated at 1000 ASA). In colour I work with Kodachrome 25 whenever possible, though in England the weather does not allow this as frequently as I would wish. I then use Kodachrome 64 and Ektachrome 200, the latter as an emergency on the dullest days.

My normal lens for action photographs is a 600 mm f/5.6, which in its long focus ED version must be one of the finest made in this length. This would normally allow me to photograph the batsman, the wicketkeeper (standing up) and the bowler if working from the direction of fine leg. A wider angle can be achieved, to include a number of slips, by using the 300 mm f/4.5 and the 400 mm f/3.5 lens. I have also used lenses up to 1200 mm – this was a monster some three feet long – which I borrowed from the West Australian newspaper in Perth to take the photograph of Andy Roberts on p.186.

Recent improvements in the design of teleconverters have made the use of these very long focal length lenses unnecessary. If I want to use a lens longer than 600 mm I attach one of the Nikon converters to the 600 mm – either the TC-14 or TC-300 – giving focal lengths of 850 mm or 1200 mm.

Black and white and colour photographs can be taken simultaneously by linking two or more cameras together electrically. Photographs can also be taken from two completely different angles by remote control. This is extremely useful when there is a possibility that the view from one of the angles will be unsatisfactory.

The prints for this book were all made on Ilford Ilfospeed paper. The colour separations were made from duplicate transparencies on Kodak Ektachrome 6121 Duplicating Film. In as much as the colour photographs are an irreplaceable historical record, I do not release the originals. The risk of damage at some stage of the publishing process is unacceptably high.

I still keep and occasionally use a rangefinder Leica M2 fitted with a 35 mm lens. This is the ideal camera for working quietly and unobtrusively, particularly in poor light. The pictures of Godfrey Evans, Eddie Paynter and Percy Fender on the way out to the Centenary Test were all made with a Leica.   **P.E.**

Index

Jim Coldham